Poetry of Presence II
More Mindfulness Poems

Poetry of Presence II
More Mindfulness Poems

∾

Phyllis Cole-Dai & Ruby R. Wilson
Editors

GRAYSON BOOKS
WEST HARTFORD, CT
GraysonBooks.com

Poetry of Presence II: More Mindfulness Poems
Copyright © 2023 Phyllis Cole-Dai and Ruby R. Wilson
ISBN: 979-8-9855442-4-4
Published by Grayson Books
West Hartford, Connecticut

Library of Congress Control Number: 201793836

Interior & Cover Design: Cindy Stewart
Cover Photo: Sascha Bosshard on Unsplash

GraysonBooks.com

Praise for *Poetry of Presence II*

"A beautiful collection of poetry that sings like music. It opens the heart and invites mindful, loving awareness into the rhythm of every part of life."

—Jack Kornfield, author of *A Path with Heart*

"*Poetry of Presence* is a gift to the soul. Each poem in this cherished collection is a meditation unto itself, a portal into the mystery of sacred awareness."

—Tara Brach, author of *Radical Acceptance* and *Trusting the Gold*

"These mindfulness poems help us wake up to the suffering of people who are different from us. That's a long process—I'll be waking up until the moment I die. But once we start to wake up, we enter the conversation on human rights. We want to tend those afflicted by the ways of this world. God was sneaky, giving us beautiful poetry to get us involved!"

—Sister Helen Prejean, leading voice for death penalty abolition, author of *Dead Man Walking and River of Fire*

"The editors understand how to present a collection of diverse poems. After all their work, they have the wisdom to pull back the curtain and let the poetry take center stage. Their generosity presents readers with a book to be savored—set on a bedside table, read in the kitchen, carried in a purse or briefcase . . . one poem at a time, let loose in our hearts and minds."

—Christina Baldwin, author of *The Seven Whispers* and *Storycatcher*

"This extraordinary collection of poems reminds us that we're not meant to live alone. It affirms what we have in common as human beings, as well as what makes us unique. It invites us, even in the midst of struggle and heartache, to choose to be present in relationship with others, offering radical acceptance, kindness, and courage."

—Rabbi Karyn Kedar, author of *Amen: Seeking Presence with Prayer, Poetry, and Mindfulness Practice*

"Looking deeply at the lives they live and encounter, these poets honor the organ donor, the worker who mops up blood and excrement from hospital floors, the startling nobility of a disabled teen . . . so many people, moments, and things we often fail to notice or turn away from. Thank you, poets, for opening our eyes and our hearts."

—Richard Brady, author of *Walking the Teacher's Path with Mindfulness: Stories for Reflection and Action*

to

Don "Da Preacha" Mayhew, Hd.H.
who sprinkles poems he loves like rose petals
as he goes, softening the path even for feet
unaware of their own aching

and

Jim Wilson,
for his steadfast love, encouragement,
support, and patience

Contents

The Invitation   17

The Poems

Untitled (You're invited to visit) *Gregory Orr*   25

The One and Only Day *Tom Hennen*   26

Why I Wake Early *Mary Oliver*   27

It Could Be *Julia M. Fehrenbacher*   28

What It's Like to Fall In Love *Heidi Seaborn*   30

Can You Hear It? *Paula Lepp*   31

Nuthatch *Kirsten Dierking*   32

Love Note to Silence *José A. Alcántara*   33

Basking *Martha Postlethwaite*   34

August Morning *Albert Garcia*   35

In the Third Month of the Pandemic,
    My Husband Goes through His Sock Drawer *Holly J. Hughes*   36

Divorce *José A. Alcántara*   37

The Healing Time *Pesha Joyce Gertler*   38

Phase One *Dilruba Ahmed*   39

Dust *Dorianne Laux*   41

Love Elegy with Busboy *Nathan McClain*   42

Shoulders *Naomi Shihab Nye*   43

The Gift *Li-Young Lee*   44

Sheltered in Place *Richard Levine*   46

Slowing Down *Ruby R. Wilson*   47

Anything, Everything *Laura Grace Weldon*   48

Cherries *Danusha Laméris*   49

Passing the Orange *Leo Dangel*   50

What You Missed That Day You Were Absent
    from Fourth Grade *Brad Aaron Modlin*   51

Addition *Carrie Newcomer*   52

Allow *Danna Faulds*   53

Thank You   *Ross Gay*   54

Ten Thousand Flowers in Spring   *Wu-Men*   55

At the New Year   *Holly Wren Spaulding*   56

Instructions to the Worker Bee   *Lucy Adkins*   57

To be of use   *Marge Piercy*   58

People Who Take Care   *Nancy Henry*   59

At the Cancer Clinic   *Ted Kooser*   60

I Tell You   Susan F. Glassmeyer   61

February 14   *Kim Addonizio*   63

Fused   *Gloria Heffernan*   64

A Voice That Calms   *Daniel Ladinsky*   65

Sunday Morning Early   *David Romtvedt*   66

Thankful for Now   *Todd Davis*   67

What Stillness   *Laura Foley*   68

How to Live Like a Water Lily   *Annette Langlois Grunseth*   69

Here Together   *W. S. Merwin*   70

Water   *Sohrab Sepehri*   71

A Valley Like This   *William Stafford*   73

Nor'easter   *James Crews*   74

The Dream's Wisdom   *Marilyn Nelson*   75

What I Learned from My Mother   *Julia Spicher Kasdorf*   76

For Everyone   *Elizabeth Brulé Farrell*   77

Neighbors   *James Crews*   78

Figures   *Dorianne Laux*   79

Remember   *Rebecca Baggett*   80

Allowables   *Nikki Giovanni*   81

Adolescent   *Teddy Macker*   82

the river between us   *Lucille Clifton*   84

Untitled (Standing outside the conference room)   *Claudia Rankine* 85

Black Boys Play the Classics   *Toi Derricotte*   86

Excuse Me   *MaryLisa DeDomenicis*   87

Alien   *Lucy Griffith*   88

Every Mourning   *Michael Kleber-Diggs*   90

Forgiveness   *Christen Careaga*   91

House of Mercury   *Fady Joudah*   93

Queens   *Barbara Crooker*   94

Halal Delicatessen   *Patrick Hicks*   96

Normal   *Reginald Harris*   97

Your Birthday   *Pat Schneider*   99

School Prayer   *Diane Ackerman*   100

Champion the Enemy's Need   *Kim Stafford*   101

For the Man Whose Son My Son Killed   *Gary Earl Ross*   102

For Warmth   *Thich Nhat Hanh*   104

Breathe   *Lynn Ungar*   105

Chorus from *The Cure at Troy*   *Seamus Heaney*   106

My Species   *Jane Hirshfield*   108

Origami Crane Tanka / Tanka de grulla Origami
    Rafael Jesús González   109

Clearing   *Martha Postlethwaite*   110

Some Advice for Clearing Brush   *Jeff Coomer*   111

Work Was His Religion   *Marjorie Saiser*   112

The Pedicure   *Annette Langlois Grunseth*   113

If You Knew   *Ellen Bass*   114

Sponge Bath   *Terri Kirby Erickson*   115

Living in the Body   *Joyce Sutphen*   116

Walking with My Delaware Grandfather   *Denise Low*   117

About Standing (in Kinship)   *Kimberly M. Blaeser*   119

You Just Never Know   *Gloria Heffernan*   120

Compassion   *James Crews*   122

New Bathing Suit   *Terri Kirby Erickson*   123

Proxy   *Gloria Heffernan*   124

Watching My Friend Pretend Her Heart Isn't Breaking
    Rosemerry Wahtola Trommer   126

While the World Burned On   *Heather Swan*   127

Go Gentle   *Linda Pastan*   129

Cold Solace   *Anna Belle Kaufman*   130

On the Day After You Left This World *Heather Swan* 132

Death *Ron Starbuck* 133

Geraniums *Linda Hogan* 135

Patriotism *Ellie Schoenfeld* 136

Feeding the Worms *Danusha Laméris* 137

Give Me This *Ada Limón* 138

U Pick *Barbara Crooker* 139

Good Bones *Maggie Smith* 140

Overheard *Ross Gay* 141

Small Kindnesses *Danusha Laméris* 142

Why I Smile at Strangers *Rosemerry Wahtola Trommer* 143

The Aunty Poem (Mi Privilege Es Tu Privilege) *Mohja Kahf* 144

The Story Wheel *Joy Harjo* 145

Detour *Ruth Feldman* 146

& So *Amanda Gorman* 147

The Distance / La Distancia *Rafael Jesús González* 148 / 149

We Were Made for This *Julia M. Fehrenbacher* 150

Ribollita *Donna Hilbert* 151

Potatoes *Lucy Adkins* 152

Trust *Thomas R. Smith* 153

Jump *Alison Luterman* 154

The Word That Is a Prayer *Ellery Akers* 155

When Giving Is All We Have *Alberto Ríos* 156

The Wild Geese *Wendell Berry* 157

Holding the Light *Stuart Kestenbaum* 158

Blessing for the Light *David Whyte* 159

Shine *Julie Cadwallader Staub* 160

Pandemic *Lynn Ungar* 161

Love and Fear in a Pandemic *Christine Stewart-Nuñez* 162

A few days after my first vaccine, *Alison Luterman* 164

when we get through this *Maya Stein* 165

Hush *Pat Schneider* 166

Belonging *Rosemerry Wahtola Trommer* 167

A Pearl of Wind *Mark Nepo*   168

An Apple Tree Was Concerned *Daniel Ladinsky*   169

Redwood Dharma *Laura Grace Weldon*   170

How surely gravity's law *Rainer Maria Rilke*   171

Limitless *Danna Faulds*   172

Elephant in the Dark *Rumi*   173

As You Fall Awake *Laura Ann Reed*   174

Blessing for Sound *David Whyte*   175

Stages *Hermann Hesse*   176

For Belonging *John O'Donohue*   177

You Are a Poem with Feet *Phyllis Cole-Dai*   178

About the Poets   181

Index of Authors and Titles   201

Permissions   209

About the Editors   221

Acknowledgments   223

The Invitation

Some poems are good medicine. They soothe our anxieties and self-doubt, restore our balance, boost our energy and strength, help us cope with stress, or even heal. Such poems we tend to keep, and share. We dog-ear their pages. We copy them down in our journals. We mull them over in times of reflection. We pass them around in book clubs, support groups and classrooms. We send them to loved ones and friends. We read them aloud to mark special days, to observe sacred days, to endure sad days. We utter them like prayers.

Many of these "good medicine" poems are *mindful*. Mindfulness is a buzzword these days, whether in health and wellness, parenting, education, the workforce, counseling, spirituality . . . but what does it mean?

Here's one way to understand it: *Mindfulness is keeping our minds and hearts where our bodies are.* Moment by moment, we sustain a deep, nonjudgmental awareness of our thoughts, emotions, physical sensations and surroundings, right where we are.

In reading this page, for example, you invest your full self in the act of reading. You're here, now, experiencing the text . . . until a moment arrives when you're not. Sooner or later, that moment will come. A sound or smell will distract you. A stray thought will lead you into a thicket of ideas. You'll be snagged by sentiment, or caught up in a rush of feeling.

That's okay. Once you notice the drift of your attention, you return to the page. *Gently.* Rather than blame or scold yourself for wandering off, you accept that it happened and bring yourself back.

We cultivate mindfulness throughout our days by returning to the present moment, again and again, without judgment. This allows us to actually live our lives instead of just going through the motions. The more mindful we become over time, the happier we are. Studies reveal that regular mindfulness practice reduces stress, promotes health, stimulates learning and creativity, enhances relationships, helps us face suffering and loss, and strengthens our compassion for others.

Many resources for mindfulness practice quote snippets of poetry or even publish entire poems. For instance, the website of the Center for Mindfulness at the University of California San Diego provides links to dozens of poems used in its Mindfulness-Based Stress Reduction classes. Meanwhile, Jon Kabat-Zinn, Sharon Salzberg, Joseph Goldstein, and other esteemed mindfulness teachers regularly invoke poetry in their books and workshops. What accounts for this popular coupling of poetry and mindfulness?

As its very appearance makes plain, poetry invites a different kind of reading than prose. The white space around the text slows us down. Like an island on the page, its shape appeals to the eye. It begs for attention. It wants to be explored, and heard. When we choose to listen, we bring the poem to life. Our voice revels in the musicality, our breath is shaped by the lines. The imagery heightens our senses. The language revives our spirits.

The act of reading a poem—any poem—can therefore become an exercise in mindfulness. And our experience of the poem is magnified when its *subject* is particularly mindful. The poem might demonstrate what mindfulness is, recount an experience of it, or offer advice on how to practice it; perhaps it fleshes out a mindfulness theme, such as acceptance, impermanence, non-clinging ("letting go"), compassion, or the unity of all things. Such *mindfulness poems* inspire us to live better, and to make our world better; at the same time, they grant us a taste of being good enough, just as we are, in this world, just as it is.

Poetry of Presence II contains nearly 140 mindfulness poems. Of course, you don't have to be interested in mindfulness to enjoy them. You can simply delight in their beautiful language, their vivid imagery, their uncommon wisdom. But if you sit down with this book in companionable silence, as with a cherished friend, the poems will teach you about mindfulness without your asking.

The poems in this collection aren't necessarily the "best" mindfulness poems out there. In the vast province of poetry, they're just ones we happen to like, and which, being skillfully crafted and highly accessible, are admirable representatives of the genre. Though their authors might never have heard of "mindfulness," they help us fathom it, and practice it. After all, it's the nature of their craft to bear witness to the *here and now*. To compose a poem, they must stop whatever else they're doing and give it their utter attention, start to finish. As Galway Kinnell once said, "[P]oetry is somebody standing up, so to speak, and saying, with as little concealment as possible, what it is for him or her to be on earth at this moment."

This volume, like the original *Poetry of Presence*, is weighted toward English-language authors from North America and Europe. They're the poets with whom we editors are best acquainted. Still, its authors speak from a rich variety of backgrounds, perspectives, and life-paths. Most are contemporary or recent poets. To some extent, all of them walk in the footsteps of great mindfulness poets of the more distant past, like Herman Hesse and Rainer Maria Rilke; or, even earlier, Rumi and Wu-Men. Older masters like these celebrated the divine presence hidden in the commonplace, or humanity's oneness with all that is. Though their worlds were vastly different from ours, their poetry still speaks to us today. We have presented a handful of their works, from gratitude.

The first *Poetry of Presence* collection betrayed our love, as editors, for natural landscapes, flora and fauna, the ever-changing sky, and the rhythm of the seasons. It also reflected our confidence in nature as an effective mindfulness teacher. Natural spaces sharpen our senses, help us tune in, and make us more aware of being alive.

It's one thing to practice mindfulness on a retreat into the mountains or an excursion along the beach. It's quite another to practice mindfulness smack dab in the middle of our busy lives, where we have hungry babies to feed, groceries to buy, a day's labor to perform, bills to pay, illnesses to endure, relationships to repair, injustices to remedy . . .

Mindfulness is tougher there. It requires clear intention. Patient discipline. Dedicated effort. So, while the first volume of *Poetry of Presence* was steeped in nature, it also presented many poems asking us to be more attentive and compassionate *right where we are* in our daily lives, accounting for the needs and wishes of others as well as our own.

That concern for what we might call relational or social mindfulness is even stronger in this second volume—for good reason. As editors, we felt compelled to select many poems appropriate to the tumult we've witnessed and, to some extent, experienced personally since the publication of the original anthology: the devastating COVID-19 pandemic; rampant economic woes; the rise of authoritarianism and intensifying political hostilities; the spread of racial and ethnic hatred; the erosion of civil and human rights, including the right to vote and women's full reproductive rights; the strife and upheaval due to climate change and natural catastrophes; the outbreak of full-blown war in Ukraine . . .

Mindfulness practice encourages us to face these challenges

without turning away. To accept that they exist. To deepen our awareness of them. To seek equanimity in the midst of them. To address them with compassion, hope, courage, and humility.

Many poems in this volume therefore delve into varieties of suffering: woundedness, illness, loss, and death; prejudice, bigotry, injustice; violence and war . . . a host of tough stuff that, frankly, most of us would rather not deal with.

But mindfulness poetry has the potential to crack open that tough stuff—one stanza, one line, even one *word* at a time. Enough light escapes through those cracks that we can edge forward when it gets dark or, if we need to, stay put a while and catch our bearings. By that light, we may begin to see more clearly and intuit more wisely how to be whoever we need to be, to go wherever we need to go, to do whatever we need to do. We're led more directly into the heart of the question that Ada Limón sets forth in the epigraph: "What is it to go to a *We* from an *I*?"

There are as many ways for mindfulness poems to crack open the tough stuff and spill out the light as there are poets. Li-Young Lee, in gently tending his wife, recounts a similar moment of tenderness he experienced as a child. Brad Aaron Modlin lists the lessons in humanness taught by Mrs. Nelson, a fourth-grade teacher. Dilruba Ahmed forgives and forgives and forgives. Julia Fehrenbacher invites us to the listening table where there is "no them—no other." Ellen Bass asks us to consider what difference it might make if we knew we'd be the last person ever to touch someone. Ted Kooser sings a praise song to the kind people at a cancer clinic. W. S. Merwin immerses us in the flood where we keep each other from being swept away. Nikki Giovanni spins a thread of connection between fear and violence. Lucille Clifton helps us see the river of race we might rather pretend isn't there. Claudia Rankine exposes us to prejudice in the workplace. Dorianne Laux confesses how sometimes we're so weary, we can't find a way to be present to what's come to greet us, even if it's God at the window . . . another example of how mindfulness poetry helps us acknowledge what's true.

Whether or not we have a formal mindfulness practice, mindfulness poetry can help us keep (or regain) our footing. It can help prepare us to act with clarity amidst confusion, with lovingkindness amidst cruelty. It can also provide a refuge, where we can recharge when we're worn down, where we can just *be*.

"The invitation of poetry," according to the poet Muriel Rukeyser, "is to bring your whole life to this moment. This moment is real, this moment is what we have . . . we are good poets inasmuch as we bring that invitation to you, and you are good readers inasmuch as you bring your whole life to the reading of the poem."

As editors, we can't say it any better. *Bring your whole life—your whole being—to the poems in this book.* If you do, you'll magnify their expressive and transformative power.

Here's one approach to reading mindfully: First, pick a poem you'd like to savor. Because the poems in this collection are either brief or can be read in self-evident segments, they make excellent texts for focusing attention. Next, situate yourself in a comfortable time and place, free of distraction. Now stop. Relax. Breathe awhile. Summon your full awareness. When you're prepared, read the text, either silently or aloud. Notice when your mind wanders, and gently call it back.

When you reach the end of the poem, sit for a spell. Don't analyze. Don't judge. Don't rush away. Just let the poem resonate, like the sounding of a bell, until it finishes with you. For now, anyhow.

We hope you'll return to both volumes of *Poetry of Presence* again and again, as to the company of old friends whose houses you may enter without knocking. Each time you drop in, let the encounter be fresh. The poems are living texts. They change, because you do. Get to know each poem on its own terms while also sensing its resonance with other works. Refrain from asking, "Do I *like* this poem? Is it better or worse than *that* one?" Just open yourself wide, like cloudless sky. Be the white space around the poem. The more welcoming you are of mindfulness poetry, and the more profoundly you engage with it, the more you'll be able to meet the world with a spirit of invitation, just as the poetry meets you.

Now the time has come to turn the page. Step into the presence of these gifted poets. They have sought love and happiness, suffered hardships and grieved losses, just like you. Journey with them into the *here and now.* Offer your full presence to each moment, the only life that truly belongs to you. As the poets say, it's enough.

Phyllis Cole-Dai and Ruby Wilson

The Poems

What is it to go to a We *from an* I?

Ada Limón

Untitled

Gregory Orr

You're invited to visit
A particular poem—
To go often enough
To become familiar
With each of its rooms;
To nose around in the attic
And explore its cellar.

Encouraged to arrive early
And greet dawn
Through various windows;
To linger long enough
To watch the shadows
Arrive toward evening.

Only a guest, yet
Welcome to stay forever.
To stay as long as you want;
As long as it gives you pleasure.

The One and Only Day

Tom Hennen

There has only ever been one day and it happens over and over. No one knows where it came from. It slides through time, the prow of a ship through sleeping water. It bumps against the shore of daylight each morning and sets sail alone in the dark at night. Sometimes under the awful glitter of stars. Sometimes into a thickly falling rain that sends the animals back to their dens and causes the woods to drip and become the color of owls.

Why I Wake Early

Mary Oliver

Hello, sun in my face.
Hello, you who make the morning
and spread it over the fields
and into the faces of the tulips
and the nodding morning glories,
and into the windows of, even, the
miserable and the crotchety—

best preacher that ever was,
dear star, that just happens
to be where you are in the universe
to keep us from ever-darkness,
to ease us with warm touching,
to hold us in the great hands of light—
good morning, good morning, good morning.

Watch, now, how I start the day
in happiness, in kindness.

It Could Be

Julia M. Fehrenbacher

a smile or a poem. Or new day light
that finds you through an open
window. Or, perhaps, remembering
that tomorrow was never promised.

It could be the scent
of baking bread, the first chill
of autumn that has you reaching
for your favorite wool sweater. Or maybe
it's the noticing of how easily
red maple becomes and lets go.

It could be taking today off
to be still, to un-know,
to notice. To practice loosening
your troubled grip
because grace can never
be gripped or grabbed.

It could be choosing
softness in a world grown hard
because you're tired of hurting
and being hurt and mercy
is the best kind of medicine.

It could be an invitation to gather
around the listening table
where every color is beautiful, where
there is no blame,
no shame, no them—no other.

It could be any of these things
or no thing at all, that remind
you that, really, only a few
things matter—

Food. Trees. Words. Love. Mostly love.

What It's Like to Fall In Love

Heidi Seaborn

I fall in love today
with the man fixing my water faucets,
how he crouches in his boots, feels
his way deftly to salve the leak.
I'm in love with dandelions & ugly bobs
& even morning glory as I yank
their roots free from this dark & luscious soil.
O I love, love the rhododendron
blushing newborn pink, love
the neighbor's rosy plum vine maple
& love the neighbor too,
how she's a dead ringer for Bette Midler
& who doesn't love Bette!
I even love her little dogs—yip & yap.
O today I fall more deeply in love
with my sweet dog, how he rouses
finch & robin from the hydrangea,
barks a greeting at passersby
& they bark back, their people
slowing to lean over our picket fence.
I am in love with strangers today.
Sun brushes foreheads & cheeks.
Shirts & baseball caps rainbow the sidewalk
& smiles curve like tulip petals splayed open.
When bicyclists ribbon yellow, fuchsia, lime
as they flash by, I call out I love you!
O I even love the houseflies flicking
the kitchen window, wanting nothing
more than to escape.

Can You Hear It?

Paula Lepp

There are days when,
although I try to open myself
to wonder, wonder just
won't be found. Or perhaps
it is more accurate to say
on those days I am simply
blind to what the world
has to offer

until I look down, and there,
beside the sidewalk,
are blades of grass completely
enrobed in ice, shimmering
in the glow of the setting sun,
and as they sway and move
into each other, if I listen,
really listen,
even they are singing
faint little bell-notes of joy.

Nuthatch

Kirsten Dierking

What if a sleek, gray-feathered nuthatch
flew from a tree and offered to perch
on your left shoulder, accompany you

on all your journeys? Nowhere fancy,
just the brief everyday walks, from garage
to house, from house to mailbox, from
the store to your car in the parking lot.

The slight pressure of small claws
clasping your skin, a flutter of wings
every so often at the edge of vision.

And what if he never asked you to be
anything? Wouldn't that be so much
nicer than being alone? So much easier
than trying to think of something to say?

Love Note to Silence

José A. Alcántara

It's impossible to stay in bed when you're around.
I love our morning tea, our walks in the woods,
listening to all your crazy stories.

I'm sorry that I don't contribute much,
that I mostly just nod and smile,
and sometimes scratch the back of my head.

But listening to you is like the shore listening to the ocean.
I'm swept clean of my detritus, my rotting organic matter,
everything tossed there by the rude and the ugly.

Here, let me grab my pen and notebook, my binoculars. Let me slip
on my coat and shoes. The sandhill cranes are passing overhead.
Let's go to the fields at the edge of town and make some noise.

Basking

Martha Postlethwaite

The moon, some say,
has such pull
that the oceans
can't resist.
But on this late autumn day,
it is the sun
that draws me
across the room.

I leave my desk
and its pile
and go.
All morning I sit
in the panel of light
that falls
on the far end
of my sofa.

My sole purpose
is to absorb
light and warmth
as it runs over my head
and down my neck,
like warm almond oil, leaving no stain.

August Morning

Albert Garcia

It's ripe, the melon
by our sink. Yellow,
bee-bitten, soft, it perfumes
the house too sweetly.
At five I wake, the air
mournful in its quiet.
My wife's eyes swim calmly
under their lids, her mouth and jaw
relaxed, different.
What is happening in the silence
of this house? Curtains
hang heavily from their rods.
Ficus leaves tremble
at my footsteps. Yet
the colors outside are perfect—
orange geranium, blue lobelia.
I wander from room to room
like a man in a museum:
wife, children, books, flowers,
melon. Such still air. Soon
the mid-morning breeze will float in
like tepid water, then hot.
How do I start this day,
I who am unsure
of how my life has happened
or how to proceed
amid this warm and steady sweetness?

In the Third Month of the Pandemic, My Husband Goes through His Sock Drawer

Holly J. Hughes

I'm still in bed when he comes in, dumps his socks on the floor,
begins to sort. *What's your goal?* I ask. *To organize or reduce?*

Both, he says, methodically matching sock to sock, pairing the cuffs,
rolling them in neat bundles while I watch. I remember when we met

how this defined him, his quiet sense of order extending even
to his drawers. My socks roamed free through dark seas,

each morning an adventure, a victory when I'd find a match.
Hard now to recall that time we needed to argue

whose way was right, an argument I never won—of course—
except in my own discreet disorder. Twenty-three years later,

we've worked out our roles: I wash the clothes, separate lights
from darks, and dump the clean, tangled wad onto the bed.

That's when he comes in, listens to the ball game as he folds
each T-shirt with practiced hands, as shopkeepers do,

helps each sock find its mate, rolls them into a ball, and lines
them up, soldiers at the ready. And twenty-three years later,

I'm not sure what it means that I'm grateful for this—for our willingness
to let each other be right, for these small compromises that keep peace,

for all the mundane ways we preserve order, for each ordinary moment
doing each ordinary thing together while outside, the world rages.

Divorce

José A. Alcántara

He has flown head first against the glass
and now lies stunned on the stone patio,
nothing moving but his quick-beating heart.
So you go to him, pick up his delicate
body and hold him in the cupped palms
of your hands. You have always known
he was beautiful, but it's only now, in his stillness,
in his vulnerability, that you see the miracle
of his being, how so much life fits in so small
a space. And so you wait, keeping him warm
against the unseasonable cold, trusting that
when the time is right, when he has recovered
both his strength and his sense of up and down,
he will gather himself, flutter once or twice,
and then rise, a streak of dazzling
color against a slowly lifting sky.

The Healing Time

Pesha Joyce Gertler

Finally on my way to yes
I bump into
all the places
where I said no
to my life
all the untended wounds
the red and purple scars
those hieroglyphs of pain
carved into my skin, my bones,
those coded messages
that send me down
the wrong street
again and again
where I find them
the old wounds
the old misdirections
and I lift them
one by one
close to my heart
and I say   holy
          holy.

Phase One

Dilruba Ahmed

For leaving the fridge open
last night, I forgive you.
For conjuring white curtains
instead of living your life.

For the seedlings that wilt, now,
in tiny pots, I forgive you.
For saying *no* first
but *yes* as an afterthought.

I forgive you for hideous visions
after childbirth, brought on by loss
of sleep. And when the baby woke
repeatedly, for your silent rebuke

in the dark, "What's your beef?"
I forgive your letting vines
overtake the garden. For fearing
your own propensity to love.

For losing, again, your bag
en route from San Francisco;
for the equally heedless drive back
on the caffeine-fueled return.

I forgive you for leaving
windows open in rain
and soaking library books
again. For putting forth

only revisions of yourself,
with punctuation worked over,
instead of the disordered truth,
I forgive you. For singing mostly

when the shower drowns
your voice. For so admiring
the drummer you failed to hear
the drum. In forgotten tin cans,

may forgiveness gather. Pooling
in gutters. Gushing from pipes.
A great steady rain of olives
from branches, relieved

of cruelty and petty meanness.
With it, a flurry of wings, thirteen
gray pigeons. Ointment reserved
for healers and prophets. I forgive you.

I forgive you. For feeling awkward
and nervous without reason.
For bearing Keats's empty vessel
with such calm you worried

you had, perhaps, no moral
center at all. For treating your mother
with contempt when she deserved
compassion. I forgive you. I forgive

you. I forgive you. For growing
a capacity for love that is great
but matched only, perhaps,
by your loneliness. For being unable

to forgive yourself first so you
could then forgive others and
at last find a way to become
the love that you want in this world.

Dust

Dorianne Laux

Someone spoke to me last night,
told me the truth. Just a few words,
but I recognized it.
I knew I should make myself get up,
write it down, but it was late,
and I was exhausted from working
all day in the garden, moving rocks.
Now, I remember only the flavor—
not like food, sweet or sharp.
More like a fine powder, like dust.
And I wasn't elated or frightened,
but simply rapt, aware.
That's how it is sometimes—
God comes to your window,
all bright light and black wings,
and you're just too tired to open it.

Love Elegy with Busboy

Nathan McClain

The whole mess—
pair of chopsticks pulled apart,
tarnished pot of tea,
even my fortune
(which was no good)—
we left for the busboy to clear.
I'd probably feel more
guilty if he didn't
so beautifully sweep our soiled plates
into his plastic black tub
and the strewn rice into his palm.
The salt and pepper shakers
were set next to each other again.
A new candle was lit.
You'd never know
how reckless we'd been,
how much we'd ruined.
With the table now so spotless,
who's to say we couldn't just go
back? Who says we can't start over,
if we want?

Shoulders

Naomi Shihab Nye

A man crosses the street in rain,
stepping gently, looking two times north and south,
because his son is asleep on his shoulder.

No car must splash him.
No car drive too near to his shadow.

This man carries the world's most sensitive cargo
but he's not marked.
Nowhere does his jacket say FRAGILE,
HANDLE WITH CARE.

His ear fills up with breathing.
He hears the hum of a boy's dream
deep inside him.

We're not going to be able
to live in this world
if we're not willing to do what he's doing
with one another.

The road will only be wide.
The rain will never stop falling.

The Gift

Li-Young Lee

To pull the metal splinter from my palm
my father recited a story in a low voice.
I watched his lovely face and not the blade.
Before the story ended, he'd removed
the iron sliver I thought I'd die from.

I can't remember the tale,
but hear his voice still, a well
of dark water, a prayer.
And I recall his hands,
two measures of tenderness
he laid against my face,
the flames of discipline
he raised above my head.

Had you entered that afternoon
you would have thought you saw a man
planting something in a boy's palm,
a silver tear, a tiny flame.
Had you followed that boy
you would have arrived here,
where I bend over my wife's right hand.

Look how I shave her thumbnail down
so carefully she feels no pain.
Watch as I lift the splinter out.
I was seven when my father
took my hand like this,
and I did not hold that shard
between my fingers and think,
Metal that will bury me,
christen it Little Assassin,
Ore Going Deep for My Heart.
And I did not lift up my wound and cry,

Death visited here!
I did what a child does
when he's given something to keep.
I kissed my father.

Sheltered in Place

Richard Levine

You watch your boy struggle with giving
up the turtle, returning it to the pond
where he'd found it on a walk—
first time you'd all been out in days.

How thoughtful he thought he'd been,
making it a home in the home
where the family sheltered in place.
How he cared for his armored friend.

Having picked flowers, knowing they'd die,
you understand the urge to pluck
the exotic, the beautiful—any diversion
from fear, which is in itself a disease.

That morning, you helped your boy
give up the idea of living forever.

Slowing Down

Ruby R. Wilson

I'm in a hurry
when I decide to slow down
and walk behind an elderly woman
creeping toward the store entrance.

I'd say the guy is in his thirties
with tattooed arms and a chain
securing his billfold to his pants.
Wearing biker boots and no mask,
he cuts in front of both of us
and strides past the employee
posted at the door
to remind customers
of the mask policy.

He is ahead of me again
in the pharmacy line,
still without a mask.
He's the age of my sons.
He was a baby once,
adored by his mother,
cradled in her arms,
the boy who is still there
inside the man,
somewhere underneath
all those thick, tough
layers of skin.

Anything, Everything

Laura Grace Weldon

"Find everything you're looking for?" a clerk asks
and I say, "I'm still looking for world peace."
"Can I get you anything else?" a nurse asks
and I say, "Yes, a safe haven for refugees."
For a millisecond, their faces soften
as they take a deep breath of imagining
then laugh or shake their heads
or commiserate. For a few minutes
we might even discuss
our planet's highest possibilities.
Maybe that deep breath,
that imagining,
 is a starting place.

Cherries

Danusha Laméris

The woman standing across the Whole Foods aisle
over the pyramid of fruit, neatly arranged
under glossy lights, watched me drop
a handful into a paper bag, said *how do you do it?*
I always have to check each one.
I looked down at the dark red fruit, each cherry
good in its own, particular way
the way breasts are good or birds or stars.
Doesn't everything that shines carry its own shadow?
A scar across the surface, a worm buried in the sweet flesh.
Why not forget Death, the sharpened blade. Reach in,
take whatever falls into your hand.

Passing the Orange

Leo Dangel

On Halloween night
the new teacher gave a party
for the parents.
She lined up the women
on one side of the schoolroom,
the men on the other,
and they had a race,
passing an orange
under their chins along each line.
The women giggled like girls
and dropped their orange
before it got halfway,
but it was the men's line
that we watched.
Who would have thought
that anyone could get them
to do such a thing?
Farmers in flannel shirts,
in blue overalls and striped overalls.
Stout men embracing one another.
Our fathers passing the orange,
passing the embrace—the kiss
of peace—complaining
about each other's whiskers,
becoming a team, winning the race.

What You Missed That Day You Were Absent from Fourth Grade

Brad Aaron Modlin

Mrs. Nelson explained how to stand still and listen
to the wind, how to find meaning in pumping gas,

how peeling potatoes can be a form of prayer. She took
questions on how not to feel lost in the dark.

After lunch she distributed worksheets
that covered ways to remember your grandfather's

voice. Then the class discussed falling asleep
without feeling you had forgotten to do something else—

something important—and how to believe
the house you wake in is your home. This prompted

Mrs. Nelson to draw a chalkboard diagram detailing
how to chant the Psalms during cigarette breaks,

and how not to squirm for sound when your own thoughts
are all you hear; also, that you have enough.

The English lesson was that *I am*
is a complete sentence.

And just before the afternoon bell, she made the math equation
look easy. The one that proves that hundreds of questions,

and feeling cold, and all those nights spent looking
for whatever it was you lost, and one person

add up to something.

Addition

Carrie Newcomer

My father taught me about numbers,
How to carry forward
What had grown too large for its column
Add the 5 to the 7
Carry forward the 10
Leaving only a 2.
It is like that,
Taking all you've come through,
Combining everything gathered and lost,
Add to the sum a little kindness
For doing the best you could
With what you knew at the time.
Tally up all the fives and sevens,
All the sixes and fours,
All that came up odd or even,
Then carry forward
Your expanded self
Which has grown beyond the limits
Of the first container.
Nothing is ever truly gone;
It only changes places.

Allow

Danna Faulds

There is no controlling life.
Try corralling a lightning bolt,
containing a tornado. Dam a
stream, and it will create a new
channel. Resist, and the tide
will sweep you off your feet.
Allow, and grace will carry
you to higher ground. The only
safety lies in letting it all in—
the wild with the weak; fear,
fantasies, failures and success.
When loss rips off the doors of
the heart, or sadness veils your
vision with despair, practice
becomes simply bearing the truth.
In the choice to let go of your
known way of being, the whole
world is revealed to your new eyes.

Thank You

Ross Gay

If you find yourself half naked
and barefoot in the frosty grass, hearing,
again, the earth's great, sonorous moan that says
you are the air of the now and gone, that says
all you love will turn to dust,
and will meet you there, do not
raise your fist. Do not raise
your small voice against it. And do not
take cover. Instead, curl your toes
into the grass, watch the cloud
ascending from your lips. Walk
through the garden's dormant splendor.
Say only, thank you.
Thank you.

Ten Thousand Flowers in Spring

Wu-Men

Translated from the Chinese by Stephen Mitchell

Ten thousand flowers in spring, the moon in autumn,
a cool breeze in summer, snow in winter.
If your mind isn't clouded by unnecessary things,
this is the best season of your life.

At the New Year

Holly Wren Spaulding

Plain things please me again,
ordinary Mondays.
Bean soup in a white bowl,
firewood in my arms,
the weight of longing.
Nothing is assured
but we have survived, been lucky.
Looking up from the page
it all surprises—
piled mail, other people, the air.

Instructions to the Worker Bee

Lucy Adkins

Remember your first duty—
seeking out beauty in the world
and going within.
There is rapture in a field of clover—
purple and blue petals,
throat of honeysuckle achingly open;
and you must be drunk with love
for salvia, monarda, Marvel of Peru,
all the glories of this world.
It's not just about pollen or nectar,
the honey that eventually comes,
but the tingle of leg hair
against petal, against pistil and stamen,
the vault of each flower opening.
Learn dandelion,
learn lantana, red-lipped astilbe,
each with its own deliciousness.
Take what you need
and remember where it is in the field.
Then go back and go back
and go back again.

To be of use

Marge Piercy

The people I love the best
jump into work head first
without dallying in the shallows
and swim off with sure strokes almost out of sight.
They seem to become natives of that element,
the black sleek heads of seals
bouncing like half-submerged balls.

I love people who harness themselves, an ox to a heavy cart,
who pull like water buffalo, with massive patience,
who strain in the mud and the muck to move things forward,
who do what has to be done, again and again.

I want to be with people who submerge
in the task, who go into the fields to harvest
and work in a row and pass the bags along,
who are not parlor generals and field deserters
but move in a common rhythm
when the food must come in or the fire be put out.

The work of the world is common as mud.
Botched, it smears the hands, crumbles to dust.
But the thing worth doing well done
has a shape that satisfies, clean and evident.
Greek amphoras for wine or oil,
Hopi vases that held corn, are put in museums
but you know they were made to be used.
The pitcher cries for water to carry
and a person for work that is real.

People Who Take Care

Nancy Henry

People who take care of people
get paid less than anybody
people who take care of people
are not worth much
except to people who are
sick, old, helpless, and poor
people who take care of people
are not important to most other people
are not respected by many other people
come and go without much fuss
unless they don't show up
when needed
people who make more money
tell them what to do
never get shit on their hands
never mop vomit or wipe tears
don't stand in danger
of having plates thrown at them
sharing every cold
observing agonies
they cannot tell at home
people who take care of people
have a secret
that sees them through the double shift
that moves with them from room to room
that keeps them on the floor
sometimes they fill a hollow
no one else can fill
sometimes through the shit
and blood and tears
they go to a beautiful place, somewhere
those clean important people
have never been.

At the Cancer Clinic

Ted Kooser

She is being helped toward the open door
that leads to the examining rooms
by two young women I take to be her sisters.
Each bends to the weight of an arm
and steps with the straight, tough bearing
of courage. At what must seem to be
a great distance, a nurse holds the door,
smiling and calling encouragement.
How patient she is in the crisp white sails
of her clothes. The sick woman
peers from under her funny knit cap
to watch each foot swing scuffing forward
and take its turn under her weight.
There is no restlessness or impatience
or anger anywhere in sight. Grace
fills the clean mold of this moment
and all the shuffling magazines grow still.

I Tell You

Susan F. Glassmeyer

I could not predict the fullness
of the day. How it was enough
to stand alone without help
in the green yard at dawn.

How two geese would spin out
of the opal sun, opening my spine,
curling my head up to the sky
in an arc I took for granted.

And the lilac bush by the red
brick wall flooding the air
with its purple weight of beauty?
How it made my body swoon,

brought my arms to reach for it
without even thinking.

*

In class today a Dutch woman split
in two by a stroke—one branch
of her body a petrified silence—
walked leaning on her husband

to the treatment table, while we,
the unimpaired, looked on with envy.
How he dignified her wobble,
beheld her deformation, untied her

shoe, removed the brace that stakes
her weaknesses. How he cradled
her down in his arms to the table
smoothing her hair as if they were

alone in their bed—I tell you,
his smile would have made you weep.

*

At twilight I visit my garden
where the peonies are about to burst.

Some days there will be more
flowers than the vase can hold.

February 14

Kim Addonizio

This is a valentine for the surgeons
ligating the portal veins and hepatic artery,
placing vascular clamps on the vena cava
as my brother receives a new liver.

And a valentine for each nurse;
though I don't know how many there are
leaning over him in their gauze masks,
I'm sure I have enough—as many hearts

as it takes, as much embarrassing sentiment
as anyone needs. One heart
for the sutures, one for the instruments
I don't know the names of,

and the monitors and lights,
and the gloves slippery with his blood
as the long hours pass,
as a T-tube is placed to drain the bile.

And one heart for the donor,
who never met my brother
but who understood the body as gift
and did not want to bury or burn that gift.

For that man, I can't imagine how
one heart could suffice. But I offer it.
While my brother lies sedated,
opened from sternum to groin,

I think of a dead man, being remembered
by others in their sorrow, and I offer him
these words of praise and gratitude,
oh beloved whom we did not know.

Fused

Gloria Heffernan

I could not hear the blood
entering my vein
one drop at a time all night long.

Four pints. Four donors.
Four faces I would never see.
Hands I would never touch.

I could not hear their voices—
the languages they spoke,
the prayers they prayed.

I did not know what car they drove,
or who they voted for or why.
But I knew I would die without them.

I knew the rupture in my body
would only be healed
because four strangers said yes.

And now, I cannot look
at the woman in the grocery store,
or the man who cut me off in traffic,

or the people in line at the voting booth,
without wondering,
Did you save my life?

A Voice That Calms

Daniel Ladinsky

after Rumi

A voice that calms, movements that calm,
eyes that quiet—dreams that also do the
same, and enliven too . . .

Be a precious donor of peace and hope.
Give love to all you meet,

For so many in this world are being torn
apart.

Sunday Morning Early

David Romtvedt

My daughter and I paddle identical red kayaks
across the lake. Pulling hard, we slip easily
through the water. Far from either shore
it hits me that my daughter is a young woman,
and suddenly everything is a metaphor for how
short a time we are granted on earth:
the red boats on the blue-black water,
the russet and gold of late summer's sunburnt grasses,
the empty blue sky. We stop and listen to the stillness.
I say, "It's Sunday, and here we are
in the church of the out-of-doors."
Then I wish I'd had the sense to stay quiet.
That's the trick in life—learning to leave well enough alone.

Our boats drift north to where the chirring
of grasshoppers reaches us from the rocky hills.
A clap of thunder beyond those hills. How well sound
travels over water. I want to say just the right thing,
something stronger and truer than a lame *I love you*.
I want my daughter to know that, through her, I live
a life that was closed to me before. I paddle up
beside her, lean out from the boat, and touch
her hand. I start to speak, then stop.

Thankful for Now

Todd Davis

Walking the river back home at the end
of May, locust in bloom, an oriole flitting
through dusky crowns, and the early night sky
going peach, day's late glow the color of that fruit's
flesh, dribbling down over everything, christening
my sons, the two of them walking before me
after a day of fishing, one of them placing a hand
on the other's shoulder, pointing toward a planet
that's just appeared, or the swift movement
of that yellow and black bird disappearing
into the growing dark, and now the light, pink
as a crabapple's flower, and my legs tired
from wading the higher water, and the rocks
that keep turning over, nearly spilling me
into the river, but still thankful for now
when I have enough strength to stay
a few yards behind them, loving this time
of day that shows me the breadth
of their backs, their lean, strong legs
striding, how we all go on in this cold water,
heading home to the sound of the last few
trout splashing, as mayflies float
through the shadowed riffles.

What Stillness

Laura Foley

Lily pads ripple in summer breeze,
as if they bloomed for me,
revelation-white clouds float
through a divine blue sky.
No human voices break
the stillness of this hilltop pond
where I come to forget
the foolishness of homo sapiens—
where a trout leaps up from the lake,
splashes shining down,
opens a glimpse into
whatever is below the surface.
My dog, wet from a swim,
shakes dots of sparkling light
from her dark coat, forming
a watery aura.
What sunlight does to water,
stillness does to us.

How to Live Like a Water Lily

Annette Langlois Grunseth

Wake up slowly, float in a dreamy world,
silky arms folded over your face until mid-morning,
then open wide, sun-warmed awake.
Breathe from more than one place, soft and supple.
Do not worry about today or tomorrow
or care what others think of you.
Your radiant center is tough, strong,
nourished by water and light.
Wind and wave may engulf you
but you can easily separate from submersion,
opening your face to the heavens.
Push back beads of wet darkness.
Move freely. Make white water circles until afternoon,
when you fold softly back into yourself,
drowsing in the dimming daylight.

Here Together

W. S. Merwin

These days I can see us clinging to each other
as we are swept along by the current
I am clinging to you to keep you from
being swept away and you are clinging to me
we see the shores blurring past as we hold
each other in the rushing current
the daylight rushes unheard far above us
how long will we be swept along in the daylight
how long will we cling together in the night
and where will it carry us together

Water

Sohrab Sepehri

Translated from the Persian by Jerome W. Clinton

Let's not muddy the water.
Imagine that close by a dove
is drinking from it,
or in a distant grove a finch
is washing its wings in it,
or in some village it fills a storage jar.

Let's not muddy the water.
Perhaps this flowing stream runs
by the foot of a poplar tree
and eases some heart's grief.
A dervish, perhaps,
has moistened his crust in it.

A young woman stood on its bank—
the water doubled her beauty.
Let's not muddy the water.

How delicious this water is!
How refreshing this stream!
Those people who live upstream,
how fortunate they are!
May their springs be ever fresh,
their cows always fertile!
I haven't seen their village,
But surely, God's foot is on
their threshing floor and
the moonlight there illuminates
the width of their words.
The walls are low in the village upstream.
Blue there is really blue.
When buds blossom, they know, those people.

What a village it must be!
May its streets be filled with music!

Those people by the stream
Have left it clear.
Let's not muddy the water.

A Valley Like This

William Stafford

Sometimes you look at an empty valley like this,
and suddenly the air is filled with snow.
That is the way the whole world happened—
there was nothing, and then . . .

But maybe some time you will look out and even
the mountains are gone, the world become nothing
again. What can a person do to help
bring back the world?

We have to watch it and then look at each other.
Together we hold it close and carefully
save it, like a bubble that can disappear
if we don't watch out.

Please think about this as you go on. Breathe on the world.
Hold out your hands to it. When mornings and evenings
roll along, watch how they open and close, how they
invite you to the long party that your life is.

Nor'easter

James Crews

I lay in bed this morning, worried
about the state of the world when I turned
to find a pair of headlights slicing
through the predawn darkness at the end
of our driveway, and knew my father-in-law
had come to plow us out after last night's
sudden snowstorm. *Bless you*, I said
to the cab of his truck, to his steady hands
on the wheel, marked by years of carpentry,
to cigarette smoke embedded in the seats
and steam curling up from the plastic lid
on his cup of gas station coffee. To this man
who loves us enough to make our house
his first stop, who can be counted on
even in the middle of a March nor'easter
before the sun's a wink over the mountains,
lowering his plow-blade to scrape us a path
out into the hope of a brand-new day.

The Dream's Wisdom

Marilyn Nelson

I dreamed
Mama came back
for a borrowed day.
We knew she would die again;
her heart was irrevocably set.
She was so dear to me.
I knew
a new
gentleness.

Help me greet everyone I know
with the dream's
wisdom.

What I Learned from My Mother

Julia Spicher Kasdorf

I learned from my mother how to love
the living, to have plenty of vases on hand
in case you have to rush to the hospital
with peonies cut from the lawn, black ants
still stuck to the buds. I learned to save jars
large enough to hold fruit salad for a whole
grieving household, to cube home-canned pears
and peaches, to slice through maroon grape skins
and flick out the sexual seeds with a knife point.
I learned to attend viewings even if I didn't know
the deceased, to press the moist hands
of the living, to look in their eyes and offer
sympathy, as though I understood loss even then.
I learned that whatever we say means nothing,
what anyone will remember is that we came.
I learned to believe I had the power to ease
awful pains materially like an angel.
Like a doctor, I learned to create
from another's suffering my own usefulness, and once
you know how to do this, you can never refuse.
To every house you enter, you must offer
healing: a chocolate cake you baked yourself,
the blessing of your voice, your chaste touch.

For Everyone

Elizabeth Brulé Farrell

Taking the exit to the city
you pass bleak alley ways, chic
restaurants, someone sitting

on the sidewalk stoned.
He cannot even crawl to the trash
to retrieve half eaten muffins.

He is the pavement, a part
of the scenery, a broken monument
no one sees anymore. I pause

thinking he is someone's
brother, son, father, husband,
uncle, friend, who used to belong

somewhere else but has lost
the address, the will, the mind,
and cannot move from this place.

I say hello. I try and make it
the holiest hello ever said
in a tone that really means
I know you; I love you.

Neighbors

James Crews

Where I'm from, people still wave
to each other, and if someone doesn't,
you might say of her, *She wouldn't*
wave at you to save her life—

but you try anyway, give her a smile.
This is just one of the many ways
we take care of one another, say: *I see you,*
I feel you, I know you are real. I wave

to Rick who picks up litter while walking
his black labs, Olive and Basil—
hauling donut boxes, cigarette packs
and countless beer cans out of the brush

beside the road. And I say hello
to Christy, who leaves almond croissants
in our mailbox and mason jars of fresh-
pressed apple cider on our side porch.

I stop to check in on my mother-in-law—
more like a second mother—who buys us
toothpaste when it's on sale, and calls
if an unfamiliar car is parked at our house.

We are going to have to return to this
way of life, this giving without expectation,
this loving without conditions. We need
to stand eye to eye again, and keep asking—

no matter how busy—*How are you,*
how's your wife, how's your knee?, making
this talk we insist on calling small,
though kindness is what keeps us alive.

Figures

Dorianne Laux

When he walks by an old drunk or a stumbling vet,
he stops to rummage in his pockets for change
or a stray bill, remembers the cold urge
of fifteen years ago that kept his joy trapped
in a bottle or the stained nub of a roach
passed from one set of cracked lips to another.
Their creased palms open like scrolls
toward the bright coins of light, stamped chips
of winter barter for the scraps and opiates
of this city. He won't ask and doesn't care
what his money is exchanged for: a blanket,
a pair of wrecked shoes, the harsh, sharpened
glare of a needle, or a pack of smokes.
Who can calculate the worth
of one man's pain? What they need, he figures,
can't be more than what he owes.

Remember

Rebecca Baggett

There was a time when a knock
at your door in the night
meant you should hurry to open,

to see who waited outside in need
of shelter, a stool by the wakened fire,
whatever food and drink you could offer

even if it meant hunger
for your household tomorrow—
a time hospitality was sacred.

Remember that your grandfather and grandmother
welcomed strangers at their door,
that once they found themselves far from home

with night curling over the horizon
and knocked at a door
with your future behind it.

Allowables

Nikki Giovanni

I killed a spider
Not a murderous brown recluse
Nor even a black widow
And if the truth were told this
Was only a small
Sort of papery spider
Who should have run
When I picked up the book
But she didn't
And she scared me
And I smashed her
I don't think
I'm allowed
To kill something
Because I am
Frightened

Adolescent

Teddy Macker

In the Calle Real Center parking lot
—Western Dental, Allstate, KFC—
a girl of fifteen sits on the curb

eating a turkey sandwich
engrossed by a video on her phone.
Short hair dyed-black, black makeup

around her eyes, a little spiked barbell
above one of those eyes, black jeans,
and camo shirt with a band's name on it:

The Gnarlyboys. It sounds like she's watching
a standup comic. There's duct tape on her left
black boot, a sticker of French fries on her phone.

Now she's texting, her face running
through expressions like a child in dream.
Now back to her video with sound on loud.

No headphones. I'm close to telling her
the volume's impolite, turn it down,
when she efforts herself up and walks off,

a limp collapsing every other stride,
the limp she's walked each day for years now
with tormented long-habituated dignity.

I watch her lurch down Calle Real,
past an armored truck, then a laundromat,
then a noodle joint, Weight Watchers,

Verizon Wireless. Once and for all.
Once and for all. May I put down
this knife in my heart

once and for all.

the river between us

Lucille Clifton

in the river that your father fished
my father was baptized.   it was
their hunger that defined them,

one, a man who knew he could
feed himself if it all came down,
the other a man who knew he needed help.

this is about more than color. it is
about how we learn to see ourselves.
it is about geography and memory.

it is about being poor people
in america.   it is about my father
and yours and you and me and
the river that is between us.

Untitled

Claudia Rankine

Standing outside the conference room, unseen by the two men waiting for the others to arrive, you hear one say to the other that being around black people is like watching a foreign film without translation. Because you will spend the next two hours around the round table that makes conversing easier, you consider waiting a few minutes before entering the room.

Black Boys Play the Classics

Toi Derricotte

The most popular "act" in
Penn Station
is the three black kids in ratty
sneakers & T-shirts playing
two violins and a cello—Brahms.
White men in business suits
have already dug into their pockets
as they pass and they toss in
a dollar or two without stopping.
Brown men in work-soiled khakis
stand with their mouths open,
arms crossed on their bellies
as if they themselves have always
wanted to attempt those bars.
One white boy, three, sits
cross-legged in front of his
idols—in ecstasy—
their slick, dark faces,
their thin, wiry arms,
who must begin to look
like angels!
Why does this trembling
pull us?
A: *Beneath the surface we are one.*
B: *Amazing! I did not think that they could speak this tongue.*

Excuse Me

MaryLisa DeDomenicis

Again, today, the chef says
to the new bus boy: *Load this up.*
The dishwasher door hangs open.
The chef says: *Not by hand.*
This is faster. But the bus boy
looks lost, just stands. I tell the cook:
He doesn't understand just as the boss
walks in, demands: *Go! Get the pan*
from the dining room, shoves him
toward it. But the young boy can't grasp
the command without Romero who works
the kitchen translating lunch slips
into sandwiches and English into Spanish
for his friend, whom all the workers call
The Mexican. When his wife calls
they hand him the phone from a distance.
Then? They wash the phone after him.
Head down, he looks at no one.
Go tell the Mexican we need more
silverware. Go. Tell the Mexican: change
the trash. Finally, when every worker
gathers all at one time in the kitchen,
I ask the bus boy's friend, Romero:
What is his name? I say, *Say it out loud.*
We write it out on a paper placemat:
es-EEDRO, and hang it on the wall.
Now everyone knows. They say Icidro,
take out the trash. Icidro we need you
to sweep. And Icidro looks up, speaks
his first English phrase as he passes by,
smiles, whispers: *'Scuse me. 'Scuse me.*

Alien

Lucy Griffith

Summer in San Antonio,
a crescendo of cicadas,
sighs of mourning doves,
the occasional sonic boom.

An ice cream truck perseverates
around the block.
I flag him down for a bomb pop.
I smell like root beer.

The doorbell rings. Incarnación
has come to do the backyard. *En Español,*
we chat about his goats, as
I let him in, take him through.

The house smells of Marta's beans nestled back
of the stove. She's rolling balls of masa.
I lean against her thigh.
Querida, she murmurs.

Dark skinned from sun,
I am barefoot,
tough feet from tarpatch standing contests.
I outlast the boys.

So hot. I pour lemonade
for Incarnación.
Mother stops me at the door, says—
"Water is fine. Use a jar."

I wait until she retreats upstairs.
From the china cabinet, I pick the best crystal,
lever the metal tray to free the ice,
deliver *limonada* to my friend.

We sit on prickly grass,
under the pecans.

Every Mourning

Michael Kleber-Diggs

Morning: walking my neighborhood, I come upon a colony
of ants busy at work. I take care not to step on any and miss

them all, then encounter up a ways a fellow traveler greeting
the day. I am frightening her. No. She is afraid of me.

Is she an introvert? Is she a neighbor? Is she just in from the 'burbs,
from the country? Is she scared of the inner city? Am I the inner city?

Is she racist? Shouldn't I be the wary one? Or is she a survivor
like me? It can't be what I'm wearing: khakis, a blue and white

checkered button-down shirt, and the nylon sandals I favor
because they're comfortable, my feet can breathe in them.

Dear friends, I am the nicest man on earth.

And I want to shout, *Morning!* But just then a weaver or
carpenter, just then a pharaoh or fire or pavement, just

then a little black ant struggles by alone, alone. And
in that moment, I want us to give ourselves over

to industry, carry the weight of the day together, lighten
it. I want to be a part of a colony where I feel easy

walking around. Cool as the goddamn breeze. Where
I can breathe, build structures sturdier and grander

than this—but the woman crosses to the other side
of the street, and I do what I usually do: retreat into

myself as far as I can, then send out whatever's left.

Forgiveness

Christen Careaga

after Lynn Ungar's "The Way It Is"

One morning,
I'll wake up to find
I'm not mad anymore.
That the anger I'd stoked
and attended to like a fire,
like a flame my life depended on,
isn't necessary.

As early sun enters my room
with streamers of light,
I'll be surprised to find
I have forgiven you.

The tender part of me you hurt,
maybe hurt without realizing,
is not so inflamed.
It used to throb
like sliver under skin,
red and unavoidable.

And now, this daybreak,
it seems to have worked itself
out of me.
I didn't even notice.

The body has a way of doing that
if we just step aside.

When I think of you that morning,
it will be with only good wishes,

recalling how kind you are,
how brilliant,
how full of promise.

I will see clearly then.

House of Mercury

Fady Joudah

The storm funneled through town with destructive intent.
Fractured tree limbs, toppled fences, ripped shingles
like tufts of hair. Dad woke up to snaps and creaks,
the two live oaks in the front yard,
but in the backyard the nearly uprooted fig tree
brought him to tears. In the morning
two neighbors, one Black, one White
came over to bandage the oaks after debridement.
A third, an Indian, stabilized the fig tree,
pitched it like a tent with rope and stake.
On the second day, I cut up the rest of the branches,
deepened the earth for the fig, enjoyed a long lazy
lunch with my parents, and on the way home heard
a radio report on whether the sky is bluer
during a pandemic. The third day
I took my son and daughter back,
we bundled up the heaps, nursed the flower beds,
delighted in another languid lunch,
hummus, falafel, shakshuka
followed by tea and stories about fear
that comes to nothing. The kids said it was the best falafel
they'd ever had. And Mom said that going forward
her morning glories will get the light they deserve.

Queens

Barbara Crooker

> *We are all just walking each other home.*
> —Ram Dass

I hadn't taken the subway in fifty years, not since
I was an undergraduate, and I was nervous.

Back then, it was hard to navigate, as graffiti and peace
signs covered up the maps. But a friend from Queens

wanted to meet for lunch, so I took a deep breath
and set out, clutching the email she'd sent with directions.

Of course, now the maps are electronic, not readily
broken, and easy to read. But her station *was* confusing,

a maze of underground passages, and she'd warned me
I'd have to walk some distance if I went up the wrong

stairs. So I stood there, trying to align her text, match
her words to the nearby stores. An elderly East Asian

woman asked, *You lost?* She snatched the papers
from my hand. *Okay. Follow me.* Wielding her cane

like a weapon, she pushed pedestrians out of the way,
held it up like a banner as we crossed against the light.

She pointed out the "good" fruit stands, wagged her finger
at the "bad" ones, ignored the storefronts with elaborate

gold jewelry. She was my Italian grandmother, in a different skin.
When we reached my destination, she gave me back my papers.

Turn here. Friend lives there. And when I turned to thank her, she was gone. Above, in the stunted city trees: the wind through

the leaves, the sound of rustling wings.

Halal Delicatessen

Patrick Hicks

after the London bombings of July 7, 2005

The owner who made my falafel was gruff,
my smile and small talk lost in a desert.
But when his son, speaking a language I did not know,
came around the counter and tugged my jeans,
I gave him my full attention.
He pointed at meat and salad,
saying the words that made them real.

I got down on one knee and pointed at trays,
which brought a feast of words to his lips.
He reached for my hand,
and tugged me into his kingdom.
Diced apples became *tofah*, bread was *khobez*,
he pointed at ice cream, *helu*, and his eyes bloomed.

If only it were this easy, always.

I thought of him as a grown man, oblivious
to this moment of him that I will carry.
Later, we might pass each other on the street,
but today, I am the anchor of his universe.

His father wrapped my sandwich and, pausing,
passed two bottles of water into my hands.
"Hot today. You take these."

His son looked on and pointed, *ma'a*,
he said, *ma'a*, of which we are all made.

Normal

Reginald Harris

for Shara McCallum

walk long enough
with a pebble in your shoe
and walking with a pebble becomes
normal

you no longer notice
the discomfort   the limp is just
another thing to live with
pain just another fact of life

until someone you haven't seen for a time
asks   *Why are you limping*
and you remember
Oh yes, that's right—
I have a pebble in my shoe

and then what do you do
take it out   leave it in because
you are used to its dull and constant ache
do not want to learn how to walk properly again

live long enough
with war
and it becomes
normal

men and women you don't know—
someone else's children—
fly off the edges of the map
to places you were never taught existed

photos of the dead close out
nightly news programs   a familiar tag-
line as the anchor signs off
until tomorrow

images of troops march across
a strange topography   the sound of guns
going off in places so distant
you hardly notice   one barely hears a noise

until someone says
We've been at war my entire adult life
and you remember
Oh, yes, that's right—
there IS a war still going on

And then what do you do?

Your Birthday

Pat Schneider

for my son Paul, born 9/11/62

This day dawns as it has always dawned
from the beginning of time.
Oceans carry the song of whales
and tumble onto every shore
the shells of precious little lives.
We who wander here
in leaf-fall, acorn-fall September,
remember, but cannot understand
the singing, or the loss of lives.

You came bloody into this bloody world,
this singing world, this world
where war and peace forever
hold each other in a lovers' knot.

Whatever we are, we are not made for war.
War is a wound that forces us to see
ourselves; hungry for peace, delicate
in our fragile shells, and beautiful.
So are you, born on this day, beautiful.
In the deep could you hear the singing?
Its meaning is beyond what can be spoken.
Perhaps, like peace, it is a mystery
that springs unbidden out of what is broken.

School Prayer

Diane Ackerman

In the name of daybreak
and the eyelids of morning
and the wayfaring moon
and the night when it departs,

I swear I will not dishonor
my soul with hatred,
but offer myself humbly
as a guardian of nature,
as a healer of misery,
as a messenger of wonder,
as an architect of peace.

In the name of the sun and its mirrors
and the day that embraces it
and the cloud veils drawn over it
and the uttermost night
and the male and the female
and the plants bursting with seed
and the crowning seasons
of the firefly and the apple,

I will honor all life
—wherever and in whatever form
it may dwell—on Earth my home,
and in the mansions of the stars.

Champion the Enemy's Need

Kim Stafford

Ask about your enemy's wounds and scars.
Seek his hidden cause of trouble.
Feed your enemy's children.
Learn their word for *home*.

Repair their well.
Learn their sorrow's history.
Trace their lineage of the good.
Ask them for a song.

Make tea. Break bread.

For the Man Whose Son My Son Killed

Gary Earl Ross

You must understand this: my son
called me after his first firefight,
distraught that he had taken life
when I had taught him to cherish it.
He called me, said he felt weird
and needed to talk to somebody.
Who better than the father who
carried him in a backpack, read
him a bedtime story each night,
and would always love him?
I'm here, I said. Tell me about it.
He did, and I listened, offering
mmm-hmms and *yesses* and words
of comfort when his voice caught.

Afterward he felt better and returned
to his duties in this dubious war.
Meanwhile, I was relieved he had
survived another day of the insanity.
On his second tour his vehicle hit a
roadside bomb. Bleeding from his
eyes because of a concussion, he flew
to the military hospital in Germany and
later came home. Again I was relieved.
Today, on the first leg of his third trip
to the Twilight Zone we've made of
your home, he called. I was glad to hear
his voice. Glad every damn time, ever-
terrified your experience will be mine.

Later, when NPR broadcast a wailing
Iraqi father who'd lost two sons in this
chaos, I thought of you for the first time,
wondered if you were that father. It was

purely chance that your son aimed at mine
and mine squeezed off an auto-burst first.
Two—no, three fathers in agony because
our leaders are all fools. Still, someone
should recognize your pain. I do, sir,
and so does my son, himself a father.
We are both sorry for your loss.

For Warmth

Thich Nhat Hanh

I hold my face in my two hands.
No, I am not crying.
I hold my face in my two hands
to keep the loneliness warm—
two hands protecting,
two hands nourishing,
two hands preventing
my soul from leaving me
in anger.

*A healing poem written during the Vietnam War after the bombing of Ben Tre,
when an American military man made the comment, "We had to destroy the town
in order to save it."*

Breathe

Lynn Ungar

Breathe, said the wind.

How can I breathe at a time like this,
when the air is full of the smoke
of burning tires, burning lives?

Just breathe, the wind insisted.

Easy for you to say, if the weight of
injustice is not wrapped around your throat,
cutting off all air.

I need you to breathe.

I need you to breathe.

Don't tell me to be calm
when there are so many reasons
to be angry, so much cause for despair!

I didn't say to be calm, said the wind,
I said to breathe.

We're going to need a lot of air
to make this hurricane together.

Chorus from *The Cure at Troy*

Seamus Heaney

Human beings suffer,
They torture one another,
They get hurt and get hard.
No poem or play or song
Can fully right a wrong
Inflicted or endured.

The innocent in gaols
Beat on their bars together.
A hunger-striker's father
Stands in the graveyard dumb.
The police widow in veils
Faints at the funeral home.

History says, *Don't hope*
On this side of the grave.
But then, once in a lifetime
The longed-for tidal wave
Of justice can rise up,
And hope and history rhyme.

So hope for a great sea-change
On the far side of revenge.
Believe that a further shore
Is reachable from here.
Believe in miracles
And cures and healing wells.

Call the miracle self-healing:
The utter self-revealing
Double-take of feeling.
If there's fire on the mountain
Or lightning and storm
And a god speaks from the sky

That means someone is hearing
The outcry and the birth-cry
Of new life at its term.

My Species

Jane Hirshfield

even
a small purple artichoke
boiled
in its own bittered
and darkening
waters
grows tender,
grows tender and sweet

patience, I think,
my species

keep testing the spiny leaves

the spiny heart

Origami Crane Tanka

Rafael Jesús González

It's said that if you
fold one-thousand paper cranes
your wish will come true.
For peace I would gladly spend
the rest of my days folding.

Tanka de grulla Origami

Rafael Jesús González

Se dice que si
doblas mil grullas de papel
se cumplirá tu deseo.
Por la paz felizmente me pasaría
el resto de mis días doblando.

Poet's note: I offer this poem in both English and Spanish (two stanzas, if you will). Neither text is a translation of the other. Born and raised on the US/Mexico border in El Paso/Ciudad Juárez, I grew up bicultural/bilingual and consequently heir to two muses. My work is almost all discrete pieces in two tongues, and when possible I prefer to publish it as it was written, in both Spanish and English.

Clearing

Martha Postlethwaite

Do not try to save
the whole world
or do anything grandiose.
Instead, create
a clearing
in the dense forest
of your life
and wait there
patiently,
until the song
that is yours alone to sing
falls into your open cupped hands
and you recognize and greet it.
Only then will you know
how to give yourself
to this world,
so worthy of rescue.

Some Advice for Clearing Brush

Jeff Coomer

Walk noisily to declare your presence.
The rabbits and deer will leave
as soon as they hear you coming,
but the snakes need time
to process your intentions.

Take a moment to be certain
of what you're cutting.
Many stems look alike
down close to the ground,
especially when they're young.
Look up occasionally.

Don't begrudge the wild roses
for whipping thorns across
your face and arms,
or the honeysuckle
for tangling your feet
and pulling the pruners
from your hands. You'd do
the same in their place.
Honor them with a clean cut.

Never begin when you're angry
or you might not stop
until there's nothing left
to hold the soil.

Always wear gloves
and keep your eye
on the blade.

Work Was His Religion

Marjorie Saiser

It was his remedy when he couldn't
make my mother happy,
his fondest wish. When he went
off to war (he thought he was
supposed to), he figured
that if he made it back,
things would be golden. How could they
not? Beautiful America. He found
that cheaters win
and yet he would not.
Listen, work, you were his salvation,
red white and blue, long as a
ditch to be dug. You never let up.
Listen, work, thank you, and will you
help me, too? And don't go
thinking he never had fun. He took his
kids to the rodeos: the 2:00 pm
and the 8:00 pm, on the Fourth of July.
He said he'd keep buying
my sister however many hot dogs
until she had her fill. Don't go thinking
I knew what I had. I didn't. But now I
begin to. He said his vote didn't count.
He said he was okay
anyway. He said there's more
important things than the Almighty
Dollar. He was framing up a house
when he said that, pounding a nail
deep into a two-by-four.
He hit it, America, square,
again and again.

The Pedicure

Annette Langlois Grunseth

I sling a hand towel over my shoulder,
carry a plastic tub filled
with warm water to Dad's chair.
Let's soak your feet, soften up those nails.

I lift his size 14-narrow to my knee.
He tells me about summers
on his granddad's farm in Utica,
couldn't afford shoes, went barefoot for chores.

He tells me how his arches fell
walking miles in moccasins as a golf caddy
to earn money for Dartmouth during the Depression.
Smart enough to get in but had to work his way through.

His toenails, dense as tree bark,
are too thick to fit the clippers.
I file gently.
Then, squeezing lotion into my hands

I cradle his hardened heel in my palm,
work my thumbs up his flattened arch.
He tells me flat feet and a trick knee kept him
out of combat. He qualified for Intelligence.

He tells me he advised generals, gave daily briefings
about battles in the Pacific and Europe.
After kneading my way up his leathered sole,
I rub circles into the ball of his ninety-year-old foot.

He says it's his first pedicure,
sighs at how good it feels.
Holding his history in my hands,
I don't know it's the last time.

If You Knew

Ellen Bass

What if you knew you'd be the last
to touch someone?
If you were taking tickets, for example,
at the theater, tearing them,
giving back the ragged stubs,
you might take care to touch that palm,
brush your fingertips
along the life line's crease.

When a man pulls his wheeled suitcase
too slowly through the airport, when
the car in front of me doesn't signal,
when the clerk at the pharmacy
won't say *Thank you,* I don't remember
they're going to die.

A friend told me she'd been with her aunt.
They'd just had lunch and the waiter,
a young gay man with plum black eyes,
joked as he served the coffee, kissed
her aunt's powdered cheek when they left.
Then they walked half a block and her aunt
dropped dead on the sidewalk.

How close does the dragon's spume
have to come? How wide does the crack
in heaven have to split?
What would people look like
if we could see them as they are,
soaked in honey, stung and swollen,
reckless, pinned against time?

Sponge Bath

Terri Kirby Erickson

Draped in towels,
my grandmother sits in a hard-backed
chair, a white bowl

of soapy water on the floor.
She lifts her frail arm, then rests it,

gratefully, in her daughter's palm.
Gliding a wet

washcloth, my mother's hand
becomes a cloud, and every bruise, a rain-
drenched flower.

Living in the Body

Joyce Sutphen

Body is something you need in order to stay
on this planet and you only get one.
And no matter which one you get, it will not
be satisfactory. It will not be beautiful
enough, it will not be fast enough, it will
not keep on for days at a time, but will
pull you down into a sleepy swamp and
demand apples and coffee and chocolate cake.

Body is a thing you have to carry
from one day into the next. Always the
same eyebrows over the same eyes in the same
skin when you look in the mirror, and the
same creaky knee when you get up from the
floor and the same wrist under the watchband.
The changes you can make are small and
costly—better to leave it as it is.

Body is a thing that you have to leave
eventually. You know that because you have
seen others do it, others who were once like you,
living inside their pile of bones and
flesh, smiling at you, loving you,
leaning in the doorway, talking to you
for hours and then one day they
are gone. No forwarding address.

Walking with My Delaware Grandfather

Denise Low

Walking home I feel a presence following
        and realize he is always there

that Native man with coal-black-hair who is
        my grandfather. In my first memories

he is present, mostly wordless,
        resident in the house where I was born.

My mother shows him the cleft in my chin
        identical to his. I am swaddled

and blinking in the kitchen light. So
        we are introduced. We never part.

Sometimes I forget he lodges in my house still
        the bone-house where my heart beats.

I carry his mother's framework
        a sturdy structure. I learn his birthright.

I hear his mother's teachings through
        what my mother said of her:

She kept a pot of stew on the stove
        all day for anyone to eat.

She never went to church but said
        you could be a good person anyway.

She fed hoboes during the '30s,
        her back porch a regular stop-over.

Every person has rights no matter
      what color. Be respectful.

This son of hers, my grandfather,
      still walks the streets with me.

Some twist of blood and heat still spark
      across the time bridge. Here, listen:

Air draws through these lungs made from his.
      His blood still pulses through this hand.

About Standing (in Kinship)

Kimberly M. Blaeser

We all have the same little bones in our foot
twenty-six with funny names like *navicular*.
Together they build something strong—
our foot arch a pyramid holding us up.
The bones don't get casts when they break.
We tape them—one *phalange* to its neighbor for support.
(Other things like sorrow work that way, too—
find healing in the leaning, the closeness.)
Our feet have one quarter of all the bones in our body.
Maybe we should give more honor to feet
and to all those tiny but blessed cogs in the world—
communities, the forgotten architecture of friendship.

You Just Never Know

Gloria Heffernan

My mother never practiced yoga.
She never studied comparative religions
or sought to find herself in the silence
of rustic mountain retreats.

Her mudra was a cigarette poised
between the fingers of her right hand
and a coffee cup cradled in her left.

Her mantra was simple.
With a slow exhalation,
she would bring it forth
from the silence—
"You just never know . . ."

I invoke her wisdom
when a driver cuts me off in traffic
and I want to feel compassion
instead of rage—
You just never know where he's going
or why he's racing to get there.

I seek her grace
when I feel inclined to roll my eyes
at the woman in the supermarket
holding up the line while she fumbles
with a bundle of coupons—
You just never know if her children
had enough to eat last night.

I think of her when I look at
myself in the mirror
stretching my limbs
in a sun salutation,

her voice urging me
to create space for compassion.

Compassion

James Crews

Compassion sat quietly beside me
that December night with my father
in the dim light of his ICU room,
then led me to the end of the hallway
where I bought him a bottle of Coke
I placed on his tray, unwrapping
a straw and bending the end until
it faced him. Now I see it was only
compassion that kept my voice steady
as I said goodbye to him, sensing
it would be the last time, even as nurses
hustled me out, said to go home
and get some rest. Only compassion
that made me linger by his bed,
gripping the callused hand that had
fixed so much for me over the years,
then moving that cold bottle of soda
a little closer, so he could reach it
once I was gone.

New Bathing Suit

Terri Kirby Erickson

My friend is wearing her new black bathing suit.
It came with the proper cups, made to fill
with one breast and the memory
of another—which is not to say *emptiness*—
but the fullness that comes to us, with sacrifice.
There is no one more alive than she is now,
floating like a lotus or swimming, lap after lap,
parting the turquoise, chlorine-scented water,
her arms as sturdy as wooden paddles.
And when she pulls herself from the pool,
her new suit dripping—the pulse is so strong
in her wrists and throat, a little bird
outside the window will hear it, begin to flap
its wings to the beat of her heart.

Proxy

Gloria Heffernan

The social worker who specializes in grief
kindly highlights with a yellow marker
all the boxes I need to initial in order to make it legal—
boxes followed by sentences that I don't bother to read
because I know what I am being asked to do
and the disclaimers and stipulations
won't change a thing.

So I sign.
I agree to make decisions for you
when you can no longer make them for yourself.
I will watch the finale from the best seat in the house
and be the one who decides when to stand for the ovation.
We both know where this is going, you said.
And I know how you want to get there.

How many times have we talked about this moment?
While we sat outside the ICU waiting for your mother to die.
While we visited my mother in the hospice called Center for Hope.
While we listened to the machine that breathed for my sister.
Vigils have become commonplace.
Each a rehearsal.
And now we are faced with closing night.
One single light on the stage.
A light you trust me to extinguish.

And so, I do what best friends do.
I make the calls,
hold the phone to your ear.
Witness.
And wait.

I wait until the weight of the decision
is lighter than the weight of your suffering.

Wait until it is no longer a decision
but a completion.
Wait until the waiting is over.

Watching My Friend Pretend Her Heart Isn't Breaking

Rosemerry Wahtola Trommer

On Earth, just a teaspoon of neutron star
would weigh six billion tons. Six billion tons
is equivalent to the weight of every animal
on earth, including insects. Times three.

Six billion tons sounds impossible
until I consider how it is to swallow grief—
just a teaspoon and one may as well have consumed
a neutron star. How dense it is,
how it carries inside it the memory of collapse.
How difficult it is to move then.
How impossible to believe that anything
could lift that weight.

There are many reasons to treat each other
with great tenderness. One is
the sheer miracle that we are here together
on a planet surrounded by dying stars.
One is that we cannot see
what anyone else has swallowed.

While the World Burned On

Heather Swan

for Lailah

The geese shot across the water
like a squadron, a line of them,
two feet above the surface. We were
caught in their path, my canoe
merely a shape cut out
of the gathering gray light of dusk.
We watched them coming
between lake and sky, mirror images
of their bodies just below them
as they grew larger and larger,
unwavering, passing us close enough
that the sound of their wings
pressing against the wind
left us gasping, awakened
from the spell you had cast
with your poem moments before
about your dead son—
that had us floating only
on the cavernous grief,
his bones silting in the spring,
your empty hands, my own dead
returning, while the hole
left by the virus widened
beneath us like the dark water,
and the palimpsest
of the many violences
was suddenly so clear and
we were descending.
We were out of time, meaning,
not in it, but then a breath later,
the moonlight flickered
on the surface of the water, and

that sound of wings, and we were back
in the boat, the geese pulling us forward
as they did the impossible—
not stopping, but flying on together,
though the air was thick with dread
and there was so very little light.

Go Gentle

Linda Pastan

You have grown wings of pain
and flap around the bed like a wounded gull
calling for water, calling for tea, for grapes
whose skins you cannot penetrate.
Remember when you taught me
how to swim? Let go, you said,
the lake will hold you up.
I long to say, Father let go
and death will hold you up.
Outside the fall goes on without us.
How easily the leaves give in,
I hear them on the last breath of wind,
passing this disappearing place.

Cold Solace

Anna Belle Kaufman

When my mother died,
one of her honey cakes remained in the freezer.
I couldn't bear to see it vanish,
so it waited, pardoned,
in its ice cave behind the metal trays
for two more years.

On my forty-first birthday
I chipped it out,
a rectangular resurrection,
hefted the dead weight in my palm.

Before it thawed,
I sawed, with serrated knife,
the thinnest of slices—
Jewish Eucharist.

The amber squares
with their translucent panes of walnuts
tasted—even toasted—of freezer,
of frost,
a raisined delicacy delivered up
from a deli in the underworld.

I yearned to recall life, not death—
the still body in her pink nightgown on the bed,
how I lay in the shallow cradle of the scattered sheets
after they took it away,
inhaling her scent one last time.

I close my eyes, savor a wafer of
sacred cake on my tongue and
try to taste my mother, to discern
the message she baked in these loaves

when she was too ill to eat them:

I love you.
It will end.
Leave something of sweetness
and substance
in the mouth of the world.

On the Day After You Left This World

Heather Swan

I floated out to the island
of bird bones, where
their long gone voices
now whisper in the cattails
looking for solitude, solace,
but found instead
three cranes waiting
who let me join them
there on the shore.
Night fell and we stayed, all of us,
cranes, crickets, cattails,
my broken body breathing,
and in the graying light
the breeze stroked
the cool waters of the lake
the water lapping the soil
until all of it
was not separate, all of it
became one breath.

Death

Ron Starbuck

Listen, please,
we all know this is true

death comes at
some point

for us all.
But, haven't you

wondered what
part of yourself

will go on?
And what you may remember?

Will you remember your
tenth or eleventh or twelfth birthday?

Will you remember today,
as more than just another day?

Will you remember all the
precious moments of your life?

Look at someone you love today,
for one minute,

as if you saw them for
the first time.

As if they were the first ray
of sunlight, caught by

the tender passion of your eye,
lighting up your whole world.

Geraniums

Linda Hogan

Life is burning
in everything, in red flowers
abandoned in an empty house,
the leaves nearly gone,
curtains and tenants gone,
but the flowers red and fiery
are there and singing,
let us out.
Even dying they have fire.
Imprisoned, they open,
so like our own lives blooming,
exploding, wanting out,
wanting love,
water,
wanting.
And you, with your weapons and badges
and your fear about what neighbors think
and working overtime
as if the boss will reward you,
you can't bloom that way
so open the door,
break the glass. There's fire
in those flowers. Set off the alarm.
What's a simple crime of property
when life, breath, and all
is at stake?

Patriotism

Ellie Schoenfeld

My country is this dirt
that gathers under my fingernails
when I am in the garden.
The quiet bacteria and fungi,
all the little insects and bugs
are my compatriots. They are
idealistic, always working together
for the common good.
I kneel on the earth
and pledge my allegiance
to all the dirt of the world,
to all of that soil which grows
flowers and food
for the just and unjust alike.
The soil does not care
what we think about or who we love.
It knows our true substance,
of what we are really made.
I stand my ground on this ground,
this ground which will
ultimately
recruit us all
to its side.

Feeding the Worms

Danusha Laméris

Ever since I found out that earth worms have taste buds
all over the delicate pink strings of their bodies,
I pause dropping apple peels into the compost bin, imagine
the dark, writhing ecstasy, the sweetness of apples
permeating their pores. I offer beets and parsley,
avocado, and melon, the feathery tops of carrots.

I'd always thought theirs a menial life, eyeless and hidden,
almost vulgar—though now, it seems, they bear a pleasure
so sublime, so decadent, I want to enhance it however I can,
forgetting, a moment, my place on the menu.

Give Me This

Ada Limón

I thought it was the neighbor's cat back
to clean the clock of the fledgling robins low
in their nest stuck in the dense hedge by the house
but what came was much stranger, a liquidity
moving all muscle and bristle. A groundhog
slippery and waddle thieving my tomatoes still
green in the morning's shade. I watched her
munch and stand on her haunches taking such
pleasure in the watery bites. Why am I not allowed
delight? A stranger writes to request my thoughts
on suffering. Barbed wire pulled out of the mouth,
as if demanding that I kneel to the trap of coiled
spikes used in warfare and fencing. Instead,
I watch the groundhog closer and a sound escapes
me, a small spasm of joy I did not imagine
when I woke. She is a funny creature and earnest,
and she is doing what she can to survive.

U Pick

Barbara Crooker

Hot July morning, sun a burner left on high. Raspberries,
beveled treasures; sour pie cherries, ruby globes, filling
the cardboard picking box. I'm by myself, listening to the chatter
of my neighbors in adjoining rows. Some of us are up on ladders;
some are down in the brambles and briars. We all think we're
in high heaven, after the long winter, late cold spring. If this
were a protest march, would a few be carrying opposite signs,
shouting invectives? Maybe so, but we're here in this small
orchard, sharing recipes, tips on preserves, how to make
a good pie. We cradle our baskets as if they contain unruly jewels.
And then we go our separate ways, licked by the thick tongue
of the sun, to bring some sweetness to our families,
blinking our blind eyes in the multilingual light.

Good Bones

Maggie Smith

Life is short, though I keep this from my children.
Life is short, and I've shortened mine
in a thousand delicious, ill-advised ways,
a thousand deliciously ill-advised ways
I'll keep from my children. The world is at least
fifty percent terrible, and that's a conservative
estimate, though I keep this from my children.
For every bird there is a stone thrown at a bird.
For every loved child, a child broken, bagged,
sunk in a lake. Life is short and the world
is at least half terrible, and for every kind
stranger, there is one who would break you,
though I keep this from my children. I am trying
to sell them the world. Any decent realtor,
walking you through a real shithole, chirps on
about good bones: This place could be beautiful,
right? You could make this place beautiful.

Overheard

Ross Gay

It's a beautiful day
the small man said from behind me
and I could tell he had a slight limp
from the rasp of his boot against the sidewalk
and I was slow to look at him
because I've learned to close my ears
against the voices of passersby, which is easier than closing
them to my own mind,
and although he said it I did not hear it
until he said it a second or third time
but he did, he said *It's a beautiful day* and something
in the way he pointed to the sun unfolding
between two oaks overhanging a basketball court
on 10th Street made me, too
catch hold of that light, opening my hands
to the dream of the soon blooming
and never did he say forget the crick in your neck
nor your bloody dreams; he did not say forget
the multiple shades of your mother's heartbreak,
nor the father in your city
kneeling over his bloody child,
nor the five species of bird this second become memory,
no, he said only, *It's a beautiful day*,
this tiny man
limping past me
with upturned palms
shaking his head
in disbelief.

Small Kindnesses

Danusha Laméris

I've been thinking about the way, when you walk
down a crowded aisle, people pull in their legs
to let you by. Or how strangers still say "bless you"
when someone sneezes, a leftover
from the Bubonic plague. "Don't die," we are saying.
And sometimes, when you spill lemons
from your grocery bag, someone else will help you
pick them up. Mostly, we don't want to harm each other.
We want to be handed our cup of coffee hot,
and to say thank you to the person handing it. To smile
at them and for them to smile back. For the waitress
to call us honey when she sets down the bowl of clam chowder,
and for the driver in the red pick-up truck to let us pass.
We have so little of each other, now. So far
from tribe and fire. Only these brief moments of exchange.
What if they are the true dwelling of the holy, these
fleeting temples we make together when we say, "Here,
have my seat," "Go ahead—you first," "I like your hat."

Why I Smile at Strangers

Rosemerry Wahtola Trommer

> *In difficult times, carry something beautiful in your heart.*—Blaise Pascal

And so today, I walk the streets
with vermillion maple leaves inside me,
and the deep purple of late-blooming larkspur
and the lilting praise of meadowlark.
I carry with me thin creeks with clear water
and the three-quarters moon
and the spice-warm scent of nasturtiums.
And honey in the sunlight.
And words from Neruda
and slow melodies by Erik Satie.
It is easy sometimes to believe
that everything is wrong.
That people are cruel and the world
destroyed and the end of it all
imminent. But there is yet goodness
beyond imagining—the creamy
white flesh of ripe pears
and the velvety purr of a cat in my lap
and the white smear of milky way—
I carry these things in my heart,
more certain than ever that one way
to counteract evil is to ceaselessly honor what's good
and share it, share it until
we break the choke hold of fear
and at least for a few linked moments,
we believe completely in beauty,
growing beauty, yes, beauty.

The Aunty Poem (Mi Privilege Es Tu Privilege)

Mohja Kahf

I will be your aunty in the new city
where you have not yet met a soul
Come to my table and eat
Teach me your pronouns
I will be your aunty who wires you money
wherever you are stranded in this world
missed your bus your flight
When you're passing through,
show me how to outline drama eyes like that
I will be your aunty with old-fashioned
button shirts and an ironing board
you can borrow for your interview
I will introduce you to whatever board members I know
Introduce me to your artist friends
You'll make me look good at my next meeting
You can unfold my couch
Teach me golden hip moves
I will slip you any privilege I grasp
I am your aunty for life
Here are clean sheets,
and my spare key

The Story Wheel

Joy Harjo

I leave you to your ceremony of grieving
Which is also of celebration
Given when an honored humble one
Leaves behind a trail of happiness
in the dark of human tribulation.
None of us is above the other
In this story of forever.
Though we follow that red road home,
one behind another.
There is a light breaking through the storm
And it is Buffalo hunting weather.
There you can see your mother
She is busy as she was ever
She holds up a new jingle dress, for her youngest beloved daughter.
And for her special son, a set of finely beaded gear,
All for that welcome home dance,
The most favorite of all—
when everyone finds their way back together
to dance eat and celebrate.
And tell story after story
of how they fought and played
in the story wheel
and how no one
was ever really lost at all.

Detour

Ruth Feldman

I took a long time getting here,
much of it wasted on wrong turns,
back roads riddled by ruts.
I had adventures
I never would have known
if I proceeded as the crow flies.
Super highways are so sure
of where they are going:
they arrive too soon.

A straight line isn't always
the shortest distance
between two people.
Sometimes I act as though
I'm heading somewhere else
while, imperceptibly,
I narrow the gap between you and me.
I'm not sure I'll ever
know the right way, but I don't mind
getting lost now and then.
Maps don't know everything.

& So

Amanda Gorman

It is easy to harp,
Harder to hope.

This truth, like the white-blown sky,
Can only be felt in its entirety or not at all.
The glorious was not made to be piecemeal.
Despite being drenched with dread,
This dark girl still dreams.
We smile like a sun that is never shunted.

Grief, when it goes, does so softly,
Like the exit of that breath
We just realized we clutched.

Since the world is round,
There is no way to walk away
From each other, for even then
We are coming back together.

Some distances, if allowed to grow,
Are merely the greatest proximities.

The Distance

Rafael Jesús González

The distance between us
is holy ground
to be traversed
feet bare
hands raised
     in joyous dance
so that once it is
     crossed
the tracks of our pilgrimage
shine in the darkness
& light our coming together
in a bright & steady light.

La Distancia

Rafael Jesús González

La distancia entre nosotros
es suelo sagrado
para atravesarse
con los pies desnudos
alzadas las manos
    en danza jubilosa
para que una vez
    cruzado
las huellas de nuestro peregrinaje
brillen en la oscuridad
y alumbren nuestro encuentro
con luz brillante y fija.

Poet's note: I offer this poem in both English and Spanish (two stanzas, if you will). Neither text is a translation of the other. Born and raised on the US/Mexico border in El Paso/Ciudad Juárez, I grew up bicultural/bilingual and consequently heir to two muses. My work is almost all discrete pieces in two tongues, and when possible I prefer to publish it as it was written, in both Spanish and English.

We Were Made for This

Julia M. Fehrenbacher

I want to fill this space
with words that will erase the distance
between your certainty and mine

make room under the big, empty sky
for grace to sit, move closer
until skin touches skin, eyes see eyes.

Maybe we can take a good, deep
breath, clear body and mind of all
that's come before. Promise
to pay attention, to stay—
especially when it hurts.

Maybe this time we will see
that it has nothing
to do with who we've been
or who we think we are

and everything to do with being fiercely here—
like breath is for life. *Yes,*
like that.

Maybe—perhaps, we can begin
and begin again with—*I don't know.* See
that it takes just one step *toward*
to erase the distance
that was only ever a thought.

Dinner is on the stove, will you join me?

Ribollita

Donna Hilbert

I praise the way you save
stale bread left on the shelf too long,
rinds of Parmesan tough to grate,
old greens not crisp enough
for salad, but fine for soup
re-boiled from what's on hand.
I love the way you salvage
bruised tomato, sprouting onion,
imperfect squash, laying no morsel
to mold, nothing to waste,
filling each space with aroma
of soup, saying supper, *manga!*
come eat, come safely, come home.

Potatoes

Lucy Adkins

He was traveling from Chicago
to Joliet, he said, on the expressway,
Old State Highway 59, when a
semi rollover caused a load of potatoes
to scatter across the road.

People stopped, pulled their
pickups and jeeps, their Chevy vans
and VW bugs off to the shoulder,
got out and dashed across three lanes
of traffic after Idaho russets and
Yukon Golds, reds and whites and yams.

I'd have understood if it were
a Brinks truck with flyaway twenties
and hundreds. But potatoes?
Perhaps it was the fact of
sudden bounty dropping down
in front of you, and like unexpected
grace, you must be grateful,
whatever it is that is given.

Trust

Thomas R. Smith

It's like so many other things in life
to which you must say no or yes.
So you take your car to the new mechanic.
Sometimes the best thing to do is trust.

The package left with the disreputable-looking
clerk, the check gulped by the night deposit,
the envelope passed by dozens of strangers—
all show up at their intended destinations.

The theft that could have happened doesn't.
Wind finally gets where it was going
through the snowy trees, and the river, even
when frozen, arrives at the right place.

And sometimes you sense how faithfully your life
is delivered, even though you can't read the address.

Jump

Alison Luterman

Because my car is twenty years old
and the gizmo that goes ding ding ding
when you leave the lights on
has been busted for at least a decade,
I'm always contending with a comatose battery,
always approaching strangers to ask for a jump
in Trader Joe's parking lot,
or on a deserted street in the growing dark,
where a man in a Python Green Porsche
affixes the red and black alligator clamps confidently
yet incorrectly, killing the thing altogether,
resulting in a ten p.m. call to Triple A,
an hours-long wait at a 7-11,
and a midnight ride sitting in the cab
of a tow truck whose driver had just been dumped
by his wife of eleven years
and desperately needs to talk about it.
These are the adventures you may have
if you tend to leave your lights on, as I do,
at dusk when the light is tricky, the hour
between dog and wolf the French call it,
when the distracted mind is too full of shadows
to remember what the hand did just moments ago.
By now I'm an old pro at setting up cables,
fitting black to minus, red to plus,
but I'll never get over the small miracle
of how fast it all works, the spark arcing
quicker than thought
as soon as a benefactor turns their ignition switch;
my own car springing to life again
like Sleeping Beauty after just the right kiss,
the way a smile will ricochet from a stranger's face
to my own, or one kind word
retrieve a flailing soul from the abyss.

The Word That Is a Prayer

Ellery Akers

One thing you know when you say it:
all over the earth people are saying it with you;
a child blurting it out as the seizures take her,
a woman reciting it on a cot in a hospital.
What if you take a cab through the Tenderloin:
at a street light, a man in a wool cap,
yarn unraveling across his face, knocks at the window;
he says, *Please.*
By the time you hear what he's saying,
the light changes, the cab pulls away,
and you don't go back, though you know
someone just prayed to you the way you pray.
Please: a word so short
it could get lost in the air
as it floats up to God like the feather it is,
knocking and knocking, and finally
falling back to earth as rain,
as pellets of ice, soaking a black branch,
collecting in drains, leaching into the ground,
and you walk in that weather every day.

When Giving Is All We Have

Alberto Ríos

> *One river gives*
> *Its journey to the next*

We give because someone gave to us.
We give because nobody gave to us.

We give because giving has changed us.
We give because giving could have changed us.

We have been better for it,
We have been wounded by it—

Giving has many faces: It is loud and quiet,
Big, though small, diamond in wood-nails.

Its story is old, the plot worn and the pages too,
But we read this book, anyway, over and again:

Giving is, first and every time, hand to hand,
Mine to yours, yours to mine.

You gave me blue and I gave you yellow.
Together we are simple green. You gave me

What you did not have, and I gave you
What I had to give—together, we made

Something greater from the difference.

The Wild Geese

Wendell Berry

Horseback on Sunday morning,
harvest over, we taste persimmon
and wild grape, sharp sweet
of summer's end. In time's maze
over fall fields, we name names
that went west from here, names
that rest on graves. We open
a persimmon seed to find the tree
that stands in promise,
pale, in the seed's marrow.
Geese appear high over us,
pass, and the sky closes. Abandon,
as in love or sleep, holds
them to their way, clear,
in the ancient faith: what we need
is here. And we pray, not
for new earth or heaven, but to be
quiet in heart, and in eye
clear. What we need is here.

Holding the Light

Stuart Kestenbaum

for Kait Rhoads

Gather up whatever is
glittering in the gutter,
whatever has tumbled
in the waves or fallen
in flames out of the sky,

for it's not only our
hearts that are broken,
but the heart
of the world as well.
Stitch it back together.

Make a place where
the day speaks to the night
and the earth speaks to the sky.
Whether we created God
or God created us

it all comes down to this:
In our imperfect world
we are meant to repair
and stitch together
what beauty there is, stitch it

with compassion and wire.
See how everything
we have made gathers
the light inside itself
and overflows? A blessing.

Blessing for the Light

David Whyte

I thank you, light, again,
for helping me to find
the outline of my daughter's face,
I thank you light,
for the subtle way
your merest touch gives shape
to such things I could
only learn to love
through your delicate instruction,
and I thank you, this morning
waking again,
most intimately and secretly
for your visible invisibility,
the way you make me look
at the face of the world
so that everything becomes
an eye to everything else
and so that strangely,
I also see myself being seen,
so that I can be born again
in that sight, so that
I can have this one other way
along with every other way,
to know that I am here.

Shine

Julie Cadwallader Staub

After the first bus comes and picks up
a dozen passengers, I'm alone at the bus stop

when an older man approaches me
drooling, dressed in a bright yellow crossing guard vest
his clothes stained, hanging loose from his frame

says Do you have a dollar to spare
Yes, I certainly do, I say
and reach into my bag

…such watery blue eyes he has and what makes a person drool like that…

Do you believe in God he asks
as I glance down to my wallet to avoid the ten or the five
I say, yes, I certainly do

and when I look at him again
he has straightened up, and there, beside Shelburne Road
and its four lanes of traffic in rush hour frenzy,

he makes a sweeping sign of the cross
as high as he can reach
as wide as he can stretch

and says, looking at me
God bless you
and Jesus too.

Then he takes the dollar
in his rough, misshapen hands
and walks down the block, across the street

that safety vest shining the whole way.

Pandemic

Lynn Ungar

What if you thought of it
as the Jews consider the Sabbath—
the most sacred of times?
Cease from travel.
Cease from buying and selling.
Give up, just for now,
on trying to make the world
different than it is.
Sing. Pray. Touch only those
to whom you commit your life.
Center down.

And when your body has become still,
reach out with your heart.
Know that we are connected
in ways that are terrifying and beautiful.
(You could hardly deny it now.)
Know that our lives
are in one another's hands.
(Surely, that has come clear.)
Do not reach out your hands.
Reach out your heart.
Reach out your words.
Reach out all the tendrils
of compassion that move, invisibly,
where we cannot touch.

Promise this world your love—
for better or for worse,
in sickness and in health,
so long as we all shall live.

Love and Fear in a Pandemic

Christine Stewart-Nuñez

1.
Once, when pregnant with death, heart stopped
within my womb, I realized I loved
someone I'd never meet. I draw on that
vibration as April deepens in this
rural place, folks still lifting their laughter
to the sky in large, loquacious groups.
Last night, my husband said if he takes sick
and succumbs, he'll die thinking of me, and I
realized the power of loving through time.
Elsewhere, bodies pile up, hospitals
overwhelmed, and survivors grieve.
Despite the ache and anchor of these four walls,
during the quarantine, the quarantine,
I recall love, and for now, I stay in.

2.
If not in quarantine, I wouldn't think
twice about biking through a graveyard
and pausing at the Gerber daisies strewn
across loose soil, and I wouldn't wonder if
the 90-year-old died alone—nursing
home locked down—or surrounded by family.
If not in quarantine, I wouldn't raise
an eyebrow when my four-year-old asks
if we can bike through again to see
if a body's in an open pit,
and I wouldn't drop everything to find
a kid-friendly video on burials
only to have him throw his arms around
me when it's done: I hope you don't get the virus,
Mommy. If not in quarantine, my child
wouldn't worry this way.

3.

The pandemic puts pressure on love
and presents fear with a new playground.
Love's learning to teach our sons art,
math, reading; it's cooking three meals a day
and remote working under the microscope
of one another's gaze. Unmoored, we click
on graphs, charts, photos. Testimonies
of the sick, the dead, and the survivors
shape and story our fears. Metaphor falters
when we scrutinize the data, and we can't
find beauty there. Love's reaching for
each other only to find our scars relaxed.
Inside these walls, we have food, resources,
each other—love and fear's first real test.

A few days after my first vaccine,

Alison Luterman

walking by the lake, I lose an earring
and don't even notice it at first,
overwhelmed as I am
by the new lightness.
Blocks later, my hand reaches up
to just that slight empty space
where something should be dangling.
I retrace my steps like they say to do,
past the guy jogging with his mask pulled down,
and the hijab-wearing,
stroller-pushing young mother,
and the homeless man emerging from his tent
bearing a boombox on one
muscular shoulder.
And that's where I spot it,
lying on the sidewalk,
miraculously untrampled—
small, precious found thing,
turquoise oval, encircled with beads,
given to me by one
who loves me, one
I haven't hugged in more than a year.
Tiny rescue from the sea of loss
we've been swimming in these past
thirteen months,
the way we ourselves seem to have found
a raft to grab onto
in the wake of a shipwreck so vast
we can't yet see the end of it.

when we get through this

Maya Stein

When we get through this, I want us to set a table
with all of the loaves of bread we'd practiced
in our quiet houses. I want us clutching fistfuls
of the cilantro we coaxed from our city windowsills,
and I want the nascent musicians, the ones
who learned old songs on their new ukuleles,
or warbled choruses on isolated balconies, to take
the stage together. I want all the knitted, crocheted,
stitched, and mended things pooled at our feet,
warming our ankles. I want us to greet each other
in unfamiliar languages, to tell the stories of those
who have been lost. I want us to look, in unison,
toward the world millions of miles and light-years away,
to take in what is before us, and beyond us.
I want us to wake to the magnitude of our fortune
against the smallness of our time. And then
I want us to remember this, and to keep remembering.

Hush

Pat Schneider

Hush. Slow down. Say the names of those
for whom your candle burns.
Say them into the attentive ear
of memory, or of God.
Oddly, now, either one will do.
You are no longer required to believe.
Receive the gift of listening. Belief
is as hard as a hickory nut
that cracked, holds many mansions.
The faces that you love are chalices.
Hush. Slow down. Tip the chalice,
sip the wine, and say it:
all whom I remember now are mine.

Belonging

Rosemerry Wahtola Trommer

And if it's true we are alone,
we are alone together,
the way blades of grass
are alone, but exist as a field.
Sometimes I feel it,
the green fuse that ignites us,
the wild thrum that unites us,
an inner hum that reminds us
of our shared humanity.
Just as thirty-five trillion
red blood cells join in one body
to become one blood.
Just as one hundred thirty-six thousand
notes make up one symphony.
Alone as we are, our small voices
weave into the one big conversation.
Our actions are essential
to the one infinite story
of what it is to be alive.
When we feel alone,
we belong to the grand communion
of those who sometimes feel alone—
we are the dust, the dust that hopes,
a rising of dust, a thrill of dust,
the dust that dances in the light
with all other dust, the dust
that makes the world.

A Pearl of Wind

Mark Nepo

Tell me a story, any story. Tell me
what happened or what didn't happen
or what you hope will happen. I need
signs of life to lift my head. I need some
pearl of wind to open my wing. So sing
me a song. For yourself, but let me listen.
I don't care if you're trained or shy or
can't hum a tune. Just sing anything.
It will stir my heart. We can do this
for each other, can't we?

An Apple Tree Was Concerned

Daniel Ladinsky

after Hafiz

An apple tree told me it was concerned about
a late frost and losing its gift that would help
feed a poor family close by.

And then there were the jams and lots of
apple butter that could be made in a banner
crop year

when the clouds were generous with what
fell from them and the sun rationed itself
with precision.

They can speak, trees, they can say the sweetest
things, and can even tell a joke,

but it takes special ears to hear them, ears
that have listened to people . . . with great
care.

Redwood Dharma

Laura Grace Weldon

> *Redwood trees have lived on Earth for over 240 million years.*
> *Homo sapiens, about 200 thousand.*

Despite massive size,
old growth redwood
root systems are shallow.
Trees reach 350 feet tall
yet don't topple in the strongest winds.

Each one's roots interlace
with its neighbors' roots,
creating a vast network of support
unseen on the surface.

They hold on for a thousand,
two thousand years, maybe more,
all the while showing us
how to grow up.

How surely gravity's law

Rainer Maria Rilke

Translated from the German by Anita Barrow and Joanna Macy

How surely gravity's law,
strong as an ocean current,
takes hold of the smallest thing
and pulls it toward the heart of the world.

Each thing—
each stone, blossom, child—
is held in place.
Only we, in our arrogance,
push out beyond what we each belong to
for some empty freedom.

If we surrendered
to earth's intelligence
we could rise up rooted, like trees.

Instead we entangle ourselves
in knots of our own making
and struggle, lonely and confused.

So, like children, we begin again
to learn from the things,
because they are in God's heart;
they have never left him.

This is what the things can teach us:
to fall,
patiently to trust our heaviness.
Even a bird has to do that
before he can fly.

Limitless

Danna Faulds

Sun says, "Be your own
illumination." Wren says,
"Sing your heart out,
all day long." Stream says,
"Do not stop for any
obstacle." Oak says,
"When the wind blows,
bend easily, and trust
your roots to hold."
Stars say, "What you see
is one small slice of a
single modest galaxy.
Remember that vastness
cannot be grasped by mind."
Ant says, "Small does not
mean powerless." Silence
says nothing. In the quiet,
everything comes clear.
I say, "Limitless." I say,
"Yes."

Elephant in the Dark

Rumi

Translated from the Persian by Coleman Barks and John Moyne

Some Hindus have an elephant to show.
No one here has ever seen an elephant.
They bring it at night to a dark room.

One by one, we go in the dark and come out
saying how we experience the animal.

One of us happens to touch the trunk.
"A water-pipe kind of creature."

Another, the ear. "A very strong, always moving
back and forth, fan-animal."

Another, the leg. "I find it still,
like a column on a temple."

Another touches the curved back.
"A leathery throne."

Another, the cleverest, feels the tusk.
"A rounded sword made of porcelain."
He's proud of his description.

Each of us touches one place
and understands the whole in that way.

The palm and the fingers feeling in the dark are
how the senses explore the reality of the elephant.

If each of us held a candle there,
and if we went in together,
we could see it.

As You Fall Awake

Laura Ann Reed

In the red thyme
that crawls
between stepping stones
time stops.

Bees
thrust their passion
into the promise
of tiny crimson-purple
blooms.

Where blossom
ends
and bee
begins

are the first words
of the world's lullaby—
rocked
as you fall
awake
in later years

a life
spent mostly
sound
asleep.

Blessing for Sound

David Whyte

I thank you,
for the smallest sound,
for the way my ears open
even before my eyes,
as if to remember
the way everything began
with an original, vibrant, note,
and I thank you for this
everyday original music,
always being rehearsed,
always being played,
always being remembered
as something new
and arriving, a tram line
below in the city street,
gull cries, or a ship's horn
in the distant harbour,
so that in waking I hear voices
even where there is no voice
and invitations where
there is no invitation
so that I can wake with you
by the ocean, in summer
or in the deepest seemingly
quietest winter,
and be with you
so that I can hear you
even with my eyes closed,
even with my heart closed,
even before I fully wake.

Stages

Hermann Hesse

Translated from the German by Richard and Clara Winston

As every flower fades and as all youth
Departs, so life at every stage,
So every virtue, so our grasp of truth,
Blooms in its day and may not last forever.
Since life may summon us at every age
Be ready, heart, for parting, new endeavor,
Be ready bravely and without remorse
To find new light that old ties cannot give.
In all beginnings dwells a magic force
For guarding us and helping us to live.

Serenely let us move to distant places
And let no sentiments of home detain us.
The Cosmic Spirit seeks not to restrain us
But lifts us stage by stage to wider spaces.
If we accept a home of our own making,
Familiar habit makes for indolence.
We must prepare for parting and leave-taking
Or else remain the slaves of permanence.

Even the hour of our death may send
Us speeding on to fresh and newer spaces,
And life may summon us to newer races.
So be it, heart: bid farewell without end.

For Belonging

John O'Donohue

May you listen to your longing to be free.

May the frames of your belonging be generous enough for your dreams.

May you arise each day with a voice of blessing whispering in your heart.

May you find a harmony between your soul and your life.

May the sanctuary of your soul never become haunted.

May you know the eternal longing that lives at the heart of time.

May there be kindness in your gaze when you look within.

May you never place walls between the light and yourself.

May you allow the wild beauty of the invisible world to gather you,
    mind you, and embrace you in belonging.

You Are a Poem with Feet

Phyllis Cole-Dai

Look how you move in space,
as at home on a fresh page
as upon the lips that speak
the gift of you into waiting air.

The poem you are is more
than text that can be read.

Every line of you,
every word and syllable,
every comma and period and dash,
arises from breath,
takes the shape of breath,
falls back to breath.

What is breath born from?
Where stands its house?

You begin where you do
without knowing how.
You end where you do
without knowing why.

Between beginning and ending,
you lay yourself down
on the white ground of being
and rise up to meet the world
wandering through.

If one of your lines breaks
in the middle
it is
because it must.

In this life you will often change
and be changed. This is the nature
of ink being spilled, dark
upon light, that something
unseen might be seen in relief.

About the Poets

Diane Ackerman is a poet, essayist, and naturalist. She has authored seven poetry collections, including *Origami Bridges* and *Jaguar of Sweet Laughter*. Her nonfiction includes *The Zookeeper's Wife*, which was made into a feature film, and *One Hundred Names for Love*, a finalist for the Pulitzer Prize. A resident of Ithaca, New York, she has taught at the University of Richmond, Columbia University, and Cornell University. *(dianeackerman.com)*

Kim Addonizio is the award-winning author of seven poetry collections, two novels, two story collections, and two books on writing poetry: *The Poet's Companion* (with Dorianne Laux) and *Ordinary Genius*. A new book of poems, *Now We're Getting Somewhere*, was published by W. W. Norton in 2021. *(kimaddonizio.com)*

Lucy Adkins grew up in rural Nebraska, received her undergraduate degree from Auburn University in Montgomery, Alabama, and her MFA from the University of Nebraska at Omaha. She currently lives in Lincoln. Her poetry has appeared in many journals as well as former US Poet Laureate Ted Kooser's column "American Life in Poetry." Her first chapbook, *One Life Shining*, is from Pudding House Press, and her second, *Two-Toned Dress*, was the winner of the 2019 Blue Light Press chapbook contest. She has also co-authored a book of non-fiction, *Writing in Community*, which won an "IPPY" in the Independent Publishers Book Awards.

Dilruba Ahmed is the author of *Bring Now the Angels* (Pitt Poetry Series, 2020) and, previously, *Dhaka Dust* (Graywolf Press), which won the Bakeless Prize. Her poems have appeared in numerous journals and anthologies. In January 2021, she joined the faculty at Warren Wilson College's MFA Program for Writers. *(dilrubaahmed.com)*

Ellery Akers is the author of three poetry books, including *Swerve: Environmentalism, Feminism, and Resistance*, which won Book Authority's Award for Best Environmentalism Books of All Time. She has won multiple other awards, including an IPPY Award and the Poetry International Prize. She's a writer, artist, and naturalist living on the Northern California coast, and her poetry has been featured in *The Sun*, in *The New York Times Magazine*, and on National Public Radio. *(elleryakers.com)*

José A. Alcántara is the author of *The Bitten World* (Tebot Bach, 2021). He has worked as a bookseller, mailman, commercial fisherman, electrician, baker, carpenter, studio photographer, door-to-door salesman, and math teacher. His poetry has appeared, or is forthcoming, in "American Life in Poetry," *Poetry*

Daily, Ploughshares, The Southern Review, Beloit Poetry Journal, Spillway, Rattle, and the anthologies *99 Poems for the 99%* and *America, We Call Your Name: Poems of Resistance and Resilience.* (josealcantarapoetry.com)

Rebecca Baggett is the author of *The Woman Who Lives Without Money,* winner of the Terry J. Cox Award from Regal House Publishing, and four chapbooks, including *God Puts on the Body of a Deer,* winner of the Main Street Rag Chapbook Competition. Her work appears in numerous journals and anthologies, including *New England Review, New Letters, Poetry East, The Southern Review,* and *The Sun.* She lives in Athens, Georgia.

Ellen Bass's most recent collection, *Indigo,* was published by Copper Canyon Press in 2020. Her other poetry books include *Like a Beggar, The Human Line,* and *Mules of Love.* Among her awards are fellowships from the Guggenheim Foundation, NEA, and California Arts Council, the Lambda Literary Award, and three Pushcart Prizes. A Chancellor of the Academy of American Poets, Bass founded poetry workshops at Salinas Valley State Prison and the Santa Cruz, California jails, and teaches at Pacific University. *(ellenbass.com)*

Wendell Berry is a poet, novelist, essayist and environmentalist with one primary message: Either we humans will learn to respect and live in harmony with the natural rhythms of this planet, or we will perish. He lives and farms near his Kentucky birthplace. His volumes of poetry affirm and celebrate the holiness of everyday life.

Kimberly Blaeser, past Wisconsin Poet Laureate and founding director of In-Na-Po, Indigenous Nations Poets, is the author of five poetry collections including *Copper Yearning, Apprenticed to Justice,* and *Résister en dansant/Ikwe-niimi: Dancing Resistance.* An enrolled member of the White Earth Nation, she is an Anishinaabe activist and environmentalist. She is a Professor at UW-Milwaukee and MFA faculty member for the Institute of American Indian Arts in Santa Fe. *(kblaeser.org)*

Christen Careaga is most at home in the Willamette Valley of Oregon where she has been a longtime educator, hoping to inspire teens with the love of language and all the worlds it can open. Most recently, she spends her days pursuing an MFA in poetry at Eastern Oregon University, practicing piano, and attempting to cook for her expanding, beautiful family.

Lucille Clifton (1936-2010), a prize-winning poet and author, was born Thelma Lucille Sayles in New York State. Among her poetry collections are *Blessing the Boats: New and Selected Poems 1988–2000,* which won the National Book Award. Twice nominated for the Pulitzer Prize for Poetry, she taught widely and also served as Poet Laureate for the state of Maryland (1979-1985).

Phyllis Cole-Dai began pecking away on an old manual typewriter in childhood and never stopped. She has authored or edited books in multiple genres, "writing across what divides us." Recent titles include both *Poetry of Presence* volumes, her *Staying Power* series, and her historical novel *Beneath the Same Stars*. Originally from Ohio, she now resides with her scientist-husband Jihong Cole-Dai and two cats in a 130-year-old house in Brookings, South Dakota. Son Nathan is the joy of their lives. *(phylliscoledai.com and phylliscoledai.substack.com)*

Jeff Coomer turned to poetry writing after a long career as the chief information officer for a division of a Fortune 500 company. He and his wife Susan raised two children on eighteen wooded acres in the rural countryside of central Maryland, a frequent setting for his poems. He has published two poetry collections, *A Buzzard in the Proper State of Deadness* and *A Potentially Quite Remarkable Thursday*, both with Last Leaf Press.

James Crews is editor of the best-selling anthology *How to Love the World*, which has been featured on NPR and in *The Boston Globe* and *The Washington Post*. He is the author of four poetry collections, including *Bluebird* and *Every Waking Moment*, and his poems appear in *The New York Times Magazine, Ploughshares*, and *The New Republic*. Crews teaches in the Poetry of Resilience seminars, and lives with his husband in Vermont. *(jamescrews.net)*

Barbara Crooker is a poetry editor for *Italian Americana* and author of nine books; *Some Glad Morning* (Pitt Poetry Series) is the latest. Her awards include the Best Book of Poetry 2018 from Poetry by the Sea, the WB Yeats Society of New York Award, the Thomas Merton Poetry of the Sacred Award, and three Pennsylvania Council on the Arts Fellowships. Her work appears in a variety of anthologies, including *The Bedford Introduction to Literature*. *(barbaracrooker.com)*

South Dakotan **Leo Dangel** (1941-2016) taught at Southwest Minnesota State University in Marshall, Minnesota. His collections of poetry include *Keeping between the Fences* (1981), *Old Man Brunner Country* (1987), *Hogs and Personals* (1992), *Home from the Field* (1997), *Saving Singletrees* (2013), and *The Crow on the Golden Arches* (2004).

Todd Davis is the author of seven books of poetry, most recently *Coffin Honey* (2022) and *Native Species* (2019), both published by Michigan State University Press. His writing has won the Foreword INDIES Book of the Year Bronze and Silver Awards, the Midwest Book Award, the Gwendolyn Brooks Poetry Prize, the Chautauqua Editors Prize, and the Bloomsburg University Book Prize. He teaches environmental studies at Pennsylvania State University's Altoona College. *(todddavispoet.com)*

MaryLisa DeDomenicis's latest poems have appeared in *Rattle*, *The American Journal of Poetry*, *More Challenges For the Delusional* (Diode), *Instant of Turbulence* (Moonstone Press), *Tribute to Peter Murphy* (Moonstone), *Bared* (Les Femme Folles Books), *Knocking At The Door* (Birch Bench Press), and *Rabbit Ears* (NYQ Books). Her chapbook *Almost All Red* (nominated for a Pushcart Prize by Stephen Dunn) won the Still Waters Poetry Chapbook Competition. She is a member of the South Jersey Poetry Collective.

Toi Derricotte received the Academy of American Poets' 2021 Wallace Stevens Award and the Poetry Society's 2020 Frost Medal for distinguished lifetime achievement. Among her poetry books are *I: New & Selected Poems* (2019), *The Undertaker's Daughter* (2011), and four earlier collections. Professor Emerita at the University of Pittsburgh, she co-founded Cave Canem Foundation (with Cornelius Eady) in 1996 and served on the Academy of American Poets' Board of Chancellors, 2012-2017. *(toiderricotte.com)*

Kirsten Dierking is the author of the poetry books *One Red Eye*, *Northern Oracle*, and *Tether*. She is the recipient of a McKnight Fellowship, a Minnesota State Arts Board Grant for literature, a Loft Literary Center Career Initiative Grant, a SASE/Jerome Grant, and a writing residency at the Banfill-Locke Center for the Arts. She teaches Humanities courses at Anoka-Ramsey Community College (Minnesota).

Terri Kirby Erickson is the author of six collections of poetry, including *A Sun Inside My Chest* (Press 53), winner of the 2021 International Book Award for Poetry. Her work has appeared in "American Life in Poetry," *Atlanta Review*, *Latin American Literary Review*, *Poet's Market*, *The Christian Century*, *The Sun*, *The Writer's Almanac*, and many more. Her awards include the Joy Harjo Poetry Prize and a Nautilus Silver Book Award. She lives in North Carolina. *(terrikirbyerickson.com)*

Elizabeth Brulé Farrell has been the recipient of the Louise Bogan Memorial Award for Poetry, written advertising copy, been writer-in-residence in public schools, and served as an advocate for mental health awareness. Her poems have been published in *The Paterson Literary Review*, *Poetry East*, *The Healing Muse*, *Pilgrimage*, *Except for Love: New England Poets Inspired by Donald Hall*, *Proposing on the Brooklyn Bridge*, *The Perch*, *The Awakenings Review*, *Watch My Rising*, and more.

Danna Faulds is a poet who credits the practice of meditation with giving her reliable access to a vivid inner life and creative voice. A long-term yoga practitioner and retired writer for Kripalu Center, Danna is the author of seven books of poetry: *Go In and In, One Soul, Prayers to the Infinite, From Root to*

Bloom, Limitless, Breath of Joy, and *What's True Here*, as well as the memoir *Into the Heart of Yoga*. *(dannafaulds.com)*

Julia Fehrenbacher is a poet, a teacher, and a sometimes-painter who is always looking for ways to spread a little good around in this world. She is most at home by the ocean and in the forests of the Pacific Northwest and with pen and paintbrush in hand. She lives in Corvallis, Oregon with her husband and two beautiful teenage girls. *(juliafehrenbacher.com)*

Ruth Feldman (1911–2003) dedicated her life to translating poetry from the Italian language into English, producing fifteen such volumes. She was acclaimed for her work, receiving (among other honors) a Literary Translator's Fellowship from the National Endowment for the Arts, the Raymond E. Baldwin Award, and the Italo Calvino Award. She also published five books of her original poetry.

Laura Foley is the author of seven poetry collections. *Why I Never Finished My Dissertation* received a starred Kirkus Review. Her collection *It's This* is forthcoming from Fernwood Press. Her poems have appeared in *Alaska Quarterly, Valparaiso, Poetry Society London, DMQ, Atlanta Review, JAMA*, and many other publications. Her work has been included in such anthologies as *Poetry of Presence, Healing the Divide*, and *How to Love the World*. She lives with her wife among Vermont hills. *(laurafoley.net)*

Albert Garcia has written three poetry collections: *Rainshadow, Skunk Talk*, and *A Meal Like That*. His work has been featured in Ted Kooser's column, "American Life in Poetry," on Garrison Keillor's "A Writer's Almanac," and in numerous journals. A former professor and dean at Sacramento Community College, he currently lives in Wilton, California.

Ross Gay is the author of four books of poetry: *Against Which; Bringing the Shovel Down; Be Holding*, winner of the PEN American Literary Jean Stein Award; and *Catalog of Unabashed Gratitude*, winner of the 2015 National Book Critics Circle Award and the 2016 Kingsley Tufts Poetry Award. His first collection of essays, *The Book of Delights*, was released in 2019 and was a *New York Times* bestseller. His latest collection of essays, *Inciting Joy*, was published in 2022. *(rossgay.net)*

Pesha Joyce Gertler (1933-2015) was a poet, teacher, and founder of a women's writing community. She was on the English faculty at North Seattle Community College and also taught creative writing at the University of Washington Women's Center, among other places. She was especially proud to be the inaugural Seattle Poet Populist in 2005, tasked with bringing poetry to places where it wasn't usually heard. Pudding House published her book *The Healing Place: Finally On My Way To Yes* in 2008.

Nikki Giovanni is a world-renowned, award-winning poet and one of the foremost authors of the Black Arts Movement. She has published more than two dozen volumes of poetry, essays, and edited anthologies as well as eleven illustrated children's books. Her most recent publications include *Make Me Rain: Poems & Prose* (2020); *Chasing Utopia: A Hybrid* (2013); and, as editor, *The 100 Best African American Poems* (2010). *(nikki-giovanni.com)*

Susan F. Glassmeyer is a somatic therapist and Feldenkrais Practitioner® and the co-director of the Holistic Health Center of Cincinnati. For her 2018 collection *Invisible Fish* (Dos Madres Press), she was named Ohio Poet of the Year. She has two previously published chapbooks, *Body Matters* (2010) and *Cook's Luck* (2012). Susan is a member of the Greater Cincinnati Writers League and creator of "April Gifts," a ten-year poetry project honoring National Poetry Month. *(susanglassmeyer.com)*

Rafael Jesús González taught Creative Writing & Literature at Laney College, Oakland and founded the Mexican & Latin American Studies Department. He was Poet-in-Residence at Oakland Museum of California and Oakland Public Library, 1996. Four times nominated for a Pushcart Prize, he was honored by the National Council of Teachers of English for his writing in 2003; in 2013 received a César E. Chávez Lifetime Award, and another from Berkeley in 2015. In 2017 he was named Berkeley's first Poet Laureate. *(rjgonzalez.blogspot.com)*

Amanda Gorman, born and raised in Los Angeles, is the youngest inaugural poet in US history, as well as an award-winning writer and *cum laude* graduate of Harvard University. *The Hill We Climb and Other Poems* is her debut poetry collection on hope and healing. She has performed multiple commissioned poems for "CBS This Morning" and has spoken at events and venues across the country. In 2017, she was appointed the first-ever National Youth Poet Laureate by Urban Word. *(theamandagorman.com)*

Lucy Griffith is the author of *We Make a Tiny Herd* (Main Street Rag, 2019), winner of the Wrangler Prize for Poetry as well as the Willa Literary Award for Poetry. In collaboration with wildlife photographer Kenneth Butler, she has created a collection of poems about birds, *Wingbeat Atlas*, forthcoming from FlowerSong Press. Recipient of Bread Loaf's Returning Contributor Scholarship in Poetry, she lives on a ranch in Texas. *(lucygriffithwriter.com)*

Annette Langlois Grunseth, Green Bay, Wisconsin, has published in *Wisconsin People and Ideas*, *Midwest Prairie Review*, *Dispatches Magazine*, *Portage Magazine*, and *The Poetry Box*. She has earned awards from Wisconsin Academy of Sciences, Wisconsin Fellowship of Poets, and The Mill, a Place for Writers. She has published two books and is a Pushcart Prize nominee. When not writing, she practices mindfulness kayaking or bicycling where her muse tags along just for the exercise. *(annettegrunseth.com)*

Thich Nhat Hanh (1926-2022) was a Vietnamese Buddhist monk, spiritual leader and peace activist who is revered globally for his powerful teachings and bestselling writings on mindfulness and peacemaking. Dr. Martin Luther King, Jr., nominated him for the Nobel Peace Prize in 1967. He passed away at Plum Village, his mindfulness practice center in southern France, in 2022, having published over a hundred books.

Joy Harjo, a member of the Mvskoke Nation, served three terms as the 23rd US Poet Laureate. She is also a celebrated anthologist, storyteller, musician, memoirist, playwright, and activist. Acclaimed author of nine books of poetry, her most recent is *An American Sunrise* (2019), a 2020 Oklahoma Book Award Winner. She lives in Tulsa, Oklahoma, where she is the inaugural Artist-in-Residence of the Bob Dylan Center. *(joyharjo.com)*

Reginald Harris, who lives in Brooklyn, is Director of Library and Outreach Services for Poets House in New York City. He won the 2012 Cave Canem / Northwestern University Press Poetry Prize for *Autogeography*. A Pushcart Prize Nominee, recipient of Individual Artist Awards for both poetry and fiction from the Maryland State Arts Council, and Finalist for a Lambda Literary Award and the ForeWord Book of the Year for *10 Tongues: Poems* (2002), his work has appeared in numerous publications.

Seamus Heaney (1939-2013), born in County Derry, Northern Ireland, was widely regarded as a preeminent twentieth-century poet. He was also a playwright, translator, and lecturer. Among many other awards, he received the 1995 Nobel Prize in Literature "for works of lyrical beauty and ethical depth, which exalt everyday miracles and the living past." He taught at both Oxford and Harvard.

Gloria Heffernan is the author of the poetry collection *What the Gratitude List Said to the Bucket List* (New York Quarterly Books) and *Exploring Poetry of Presence: A Companion Guide for Readers, Writers and Workshop Facilitators* (Back Porch Productions). She has written two chapbooks: *Hail to the Symptom* (Moonstone Press) and *Some of Our Parts* (Finishing Line Press). Her work appears in over eighty literary journals, including *Chautauqua*, *Magma* (UK), *Stone Canoe*, and *Columbia Review*. *(gloriaheffernan.wordpress.com)*

Tom Hennen was born into a big Dutch-Irish family in Minnesota and grew up on a farm. He began his adult work life as a letterpress and offset printer, but switched careers. He is now retired from his post as wildlife technician at the Sand Lake National Wildlife Refuge in South Dakota. A heralded "poet of the landscape" and master of the prose poem, Hennen's latest poetry collection is *Darkness Sticks to Everything* (2013).

Nancy Henry is the author of three poetry collections: *Sarx* (Moon Pie Press, 2010), *Who You Are* (Sheltering Pines, 2008) and *Our Lady of Let's All Sing* (Sheltering Pines, 2007), in addition to four chapbooks. She has contributed to numerous anthologies and journals and been nominated several times for the Pushcart Prize. She has taught at Central Maine Community College and Southern Maine Community College. She has also practiced law, primarily in the area of child advocacy.

Hermann Hesse (1877-1962) was a German novelist and poet who was awarded the Nobel Prize for Literature in 1946. While popular in his own time, especially in Germany, he became hugely influential worldwide during the 1960s countercultural movement and is now one of the most translated European authors of the 20th century. Among his best-known works are *Demian* (1919), *Siddhartha* (1922), *Steppenwolf* (1927), and *The Glass Bead Game* (1943).

Patrick Hicks is the author of *The Commandant of Lubizec*, *Adoptable*, and *The Collector of Names,* among others. His work has appeared on NPR, *The PBS NewsHour*, and "American Life in Poetry," and his first novel was selected for National Reading Group Month. He is the Writer-in-Residence at Augustana University as well as a faculty member in the MFA Program at Sierra Nevada University. He hosts the popular radio show *Poetry from Studio 47*, and his latest novel is *In the Shadow of Dora. (patrickhicks.org)*

Donna Hilbert's latest book is *Threnody* (Moon Tide Press). Earlier books include *Gravity: New & Selected Poems* (Tebot Bach). She is a monthly contributing writer to Verse-Virtual. Work has appeared in *Braided Way*, *Chiron Review*, *Sheila-Na-Gig*, *Rattle*, *Zocalo Public Square*, *One Art*, *The Los Angeles Times*, and numerous anthologies, and has been featured on *The Writer's Almanac* and *Lyric Life*. She writes and leads private workshops in Southern California, where she makes her home. *(donnahilbert.com)*

Jane Hirshfield, who lives in the San Francisco Bay Area, is an acclaimed poet, essayist, editor, translator, and educator. She has authored nine collections of poetry, most recently *Ledger* (2020), and received numerous awards. Deeply influenced by Zen Buddhism, her work consistently addresses themes of social and environmental justice, and exhibits profound empathy for the suffering of living beings.

Linda Hogan, a member of the Chickasaw Nation, is an internationally recognized public speaker and writer of poetry, fiction, and essays. Her main interests as both writer and scholar are environmental issues, indigenous spiritual traditions and cultures, and Southeastern tribal histories. In 2007 she was inducted into the Chickasaw Nation Hall of Fame. *(lindahoganwriter.com)*

Holly J. Hughes is the author of *Hold Fast* and *Sailing by Ravens,* co-author of *The Pen & the Bell: Mindful Writing in a Busy World* and editor of *Beyond Forgetting: Poetry & Prose about Alzheimer's Disease.* Her fine-art chapbook *Passings* received an American Book Award in 2017. She lives on the Olympic Peninsula, where she consults as a writing coach, directs Flying Squirrel Studio, a retreat for women writers, and co-publishes Empty Bowl Press. *(hollyjhughes.com)*

Fady Joudah is a Palestinian American physician, poet, and translator. Born in Texas to Palestinian refugees, he grew up in Libya and Saudi Arabia before returning to the US to study medicine. In addition to his award-winning poetry translations, he has authored four volumes of original poetry, including *The Earth in the Attic* (2008) and *Textu* (2014), which was written on a cell phone, with each poem being exactly 160 characters long. He lives with his family in Houston, where he works as a physician of internal medicine.

Mohja Kahf is a Syrian American poet and the author of *My Lover Feeds Me Grapefruit* (2020), among other titles. The recipient of awards from Pushcart Press, the Arkansas Arts Council, the Radius of Arab American Writers, and the Northwest Arkansas Black Democratic Caucus, she works as a professor and lives in Fayetteville, Arkansas.

Julia Spicher Kasdorf is the award-winning author of four books of poetry: *Sleeping Preacher; Eve's Striptease; Poetry in America;* and *Shale Play: Poems and Photographs from the Fracking Fields.* Among her nonfiction titles are *The Body and the Book: Writing from a Mennonite Life* and *Fixing Tradition: Joseph W. Yoder, Amish American.* Professor of English at Penn State, she also teaches in the MFA program at Chatham University. She lives in Bellefonte, Pennsylvania. *(juliakasdorf.com)*

Anna Belle Kaufman is a poet, writer, and artist. Her poems and Pushcart-nominated essays have appeared in *The Sun, Utne Reader, Calyx, The Networker,* and *Brain, Child Magazine,* as well as the *Journal of Art in Psychotherapy,* and they have been performed by the Jewish Women's Theater. She lives in the country in Northern California with her second husband, dog, and two pet goats.

Stuart Kestenbaum is the author of six collections of poems, including *Pilgrimage, House of Thanksgiving, Prayers and Run-on Sentences, Only Now, How to Start Over,* and *Things Seemed to Be Breaking.* He served as Maine's Poet Laureate from 2016-2021 and was the director of the Haystack Mountain School of Crafts in Deer Isle, Maine, for over twenty-five years. More recently, working with the Libra Foundation, he has designed and implemented a residency program for artists and writers called Monson Arts. *(stuartkestenbaum.com)*

Michael Kleber-Diggs is a poet, essayist, literary critic, and arts educator. His debut poetry collection, *Worldly Things* (Milkweed Editions, 2021), won the Max Ritvo Poetry Prize, the 2022 Hefner Heitz Kansas Book Award in Poetry, the 2022 Balcones Poetry Prize, and was a finalist for the 2022 Minnesota Book Award. His poems and essays appear in numerous journals and anthologies. *(michaelkleberdiggs.com)*

Iowa-born **Ted Kooser**, a former life insurance executive, is a Pulitzer Prize-winning poet and former US Poet Laureate. For fifteen years he edited a weekly newspaper column, "American Life in Poetry." His most recent poetry collection is *Cotton Candy: Poems Dipped Out off the Air* (2022). He is Presidential Professor Emeritus at The University of Nebraska. *(tedkooser.net)*

Daniel Ladinsky is one of the foremost English-language interpreters of the mystical poetry of the Sufi masters Hafiz and Rumi. He has produced seven best-selling books rendering the works of those poets, all published by Penguin Books, including *The Gift, Love Poems from God, A Year With Hafiz*, and *The Purity of Desire*. He resides in Taos, New Mexico, where he now enjoys writing haiku and caring for the stray animals who make their way to him. *(danielladinsky.com)*

Danusha Laméris's work has appeared in *The Best American Poetry, The New York Times, The Southern Review, Orion, The American Poetry Review*, and *Ploughshares*. Her second book, *Bonfire Opera* (University of Pittsburgh Press, 2020) was a finalist for the Paterson Poetry Prize and the winner of the Northern California Book Award in Poetry. She lives in Santa Cruz, California, and teaches private writing workshops. *(danushalameris.com)*

Dorianne Laux of Maine is the prize-winning author of six poetry collections and co-author of the celebrated text *The Poet's Companion: A Guide to the Pleasures of Writing Poetry* (W. W. Norton, 1997). She teaches poetry at North Carolina State University and is a founding faculty member of Pacific University's low residency MFA program. *(doriannelaux.com)*

Li-Young Lee was born of Chinese parents in Jakarta, Indonesia, and settled with his family in the US while a young boy. He is the author of five critically-acclaimed books of poetry, the most recent being *The Undressing* (2018). His honors include fellowships from the National Endowment for the Arts, the Lannan Foundation, and the John Simon Guggenheim Memorial Foundation. He now lives in Chicago with his wife and their two sons.

Paula Lepp was born in Mississippi and now lives in Charleston, West Virginia, with her husband and two kids. Her poetry has been published in several anthologies and online journals. Paula also curates a public poetry project, "Garage Door Poetry," in which she writes poems she loves by poets she loves on her garage door—her way of subversively introducing the beauty of poetry into her community. She is currently working on her first poetry collection.

Richard Levine's *Now in Contest* is forthcoming from Fernwood Press. A retired New York City teacher, he is also the author of *Richard Levine: Selected Poems* (FutureCycle Press, 2019), *Contiguous States* (Finishing Line Press, 2018), and five chapbooks. An Advisory Editor of BigCityLit.com, he is the recipient of the 2021 Connecticut Poetry Society Award. His review "Poetry for a Pandemic," appeared in *American Book Review* (Nov-Dec 2020), and the review "The Spoils of War" is forthcoming. *(richardlevine107.com)*

Ada Limón is the author of six books of poetry, including *The Carrying*, which won the National Book Critics Circle Award for Poetry. Limón is also the host of the critically-acclaimed poetry podcast, *The Slowdown*. Her latest book of poetry is *The Hurting Kind* (Milkweed Editions). She is the 24th Poet Laureate of the United States. *(adalimon.net)*

Denise Low, Kansas Poet Laureate 2007-09, won a Red Mountain Press Award for *Shadow Light. Jigsaw Puzzling: Essays in a Time of Pestilence* is from Meadowlark Books (2022). Other publications are a memoir, *The Turtle's Beating Heart: One Family's Story of Lenape Survival* (University of Nebraska); *Wing* (Red Mountain); *Casino Bestiary* (Spartan); and *Jackalope* (Red Mountain, fiction). She is a founding member of Indigenous Native Poets. She lives in California's Sonoma County. *(deniselow.net)*

Alison Luterman's four books of poetry are *The Largest Possible Life*, *See How We Almost Fly*, *Desire Zoo*, and *In the Time of Great Fires*. She also writes plays, musicals, song lyrics, and personal essays. She has taught in the MFA program at New College, at The Writing Salon in Berkeley, at Esalen Institute and Omega Institute, as well as in high schools, juvenile halls, and poetry festivals. *(alisonluterman.net)*

Teddy Macker is the author of the collection of poetry *This World*, voted a "Best Book of 2015" by the Englewood Review of Books. His work appears in the *Los Angeles Times*, *Orion*, *The Sun*, *Tin House*, and various anthologies. He lives with his wife and daughters on a farm in Carpinteria, California, where he maintains an orchard.

Nathan McClain is the author of *Scale* (2017) and *Previously Owned* (2022). He is a recipient of fellowships from The Frost Place, Sewanee Writers' Conference, and Bread Loaf Writers' Conference. A graduate of the MFA Program for Writers at Warren Wilson and now a Cave Canem fellow, he has published poems and prose in numerous journals. He teaches at Hampshire College and serves as Poetry Editor for *The Massachusetts Review*. *(nathanmcclain.com)*

William Stanley (W. S.) Merwin (1927-2019), a native of New York City, was a former US Poet Laureate and two-time Pulitzer Prize winner. He published more than fifty books of poetry, translation, and prose. For the last decades of his life, he resided and worked in Maui, Hawaii, where he carefully restored the tropical forest surrounding his home, an old banana plantation. His Buddhist practice and environmentalism profoundly influenced his work. *(merwinconservancy.org)*

Brad Aaron Modlin is the Reynolds Endowed Chair of Creative Writing and a professor at University of Nebraska, Kearney, where he teaches undergraduates and grad students, coordinates the visiting writer series, and keeps "healthy" snacks in his office filing cabinet. For in-person readings, he remembers comfortable shoes. On Zoom, he's barefoot. *(bradaaronmodlin.com)*

Marilyn Nelson, born in Cleveland, Ohio, is the prize-winning author or translator of more than twenty-four books. Her latest poetry collection is *Faster Than Light* (2012). She is a professor emerita of English at the University of Connecticut and was Poet Laureate of Connecticut from 2001 to 2006. She currently serves as a Chancellor of the Academy of American Poets and is Poet-in-Residence of The Poets Corner at the Cathedral of St. John the Divine. *(marilyn-nelson.com)*

Mark Nepo is a poet, spiritual teacher, and storyteller. He has published twenty-two books and recorded fifteen audio projects. In 2015, he was given a Life-Achievement Award by *AgeNation*, one of many awards he has received. Since 2017 he has been a regular columnist for *Spirituality & Health Magazine*. Recent books include *Surviving Storms* (2022); *The Book of Soul* (2020); *Drinking from the River of Light* (2019); and *More Together Than Alone* (2018). *(marknepo.com)*

Carrie Newcomer is an Emmy-winning songwriter, poet, recording artist and performer. She has been described as a "prairie mystic" by the *Boston Globe* and one who "asks all the right questions" by *Rolling Stone Magazine*. Carrie has nineteen nationally released albums on Available Light & Concord/Rounder Records, including *Until Now, The Beautiful Not Yet*. Her three books of poetry include *A Permeable Life: Poems and Essays*, and *Until Now: New Poems*. *(carrienewcomer.com* and *carrienewcomer.substack.com)*

Naomi Shihab Nye was born to a Palestinian father and an American mother. Drawing on her Palestinian American heritage, the cultural diversity of her home in Texas, and her experiences traveling and teaching in Asia, Europe, Canada, Mexico, and the Middle East, she uses her writing to attest to our shared humanity. She is the award-winning author and/or editor of more than thirty books.

John O'Donohue (1956-2008) was a priest, philosopher, and poet born in County Clare, Ireland. His numerous books of "long form, prayer-style" poetry, composed mostly in a remote cottage in Connemara, grew out of contemplative practice, rigorous academic study, and love for land and sea. After retiring from the priesthood, he devoted himself full-time to writing and a public life of speaking and advocating around the world for social justice. *(johnodonohue.com)*

Mary Oliver (1935-2019), a native of Ohio, was once acknowledged by the *New York Times* as "far and away, this country's best-selling poet." Winner of the Pulitzer Prize among many other awards, she published more than twenty volumes of poetry and a half-dozen of prose. She resided in Provincetown, Massachusetts, for over fifty years and died in Florida in 2019.

Gregory Orr, widely considered a master of short, lyric free verse, is the award-winning author of twelve collections of poetry. His most recent volume is *The Last Love Poem I Will Ever Write* (W. W. Norton, 2019). Having retired that same year from the faculty at the University of Virginia, he and his wife now divide their time between their home in Virginia and a house in the Adirondack Mountains. *(gregoryorr.net)*

Linda Pastan (1932-2023), a native of New York City, resided for most of her life in Potomac, Maryland. Her quiet lyrics delved into everyday life and often the darkness and anxieties lying just beneath its surface. Much decorated, she published seventeen books of poetry and was also an essayist. Her last poetry collection was *Almost an Elegy: New and Later Selected Poems* (W. W. Norton, 2022).

Marge Piercy, born into a working-class family in Detroit, Michigan, is a poet, novelist, essayist, and activist. Her work is grounded in feminism, Jewish spirituality, and concern for social injustice. In addition to seventeen novels, she has published twenty books of poetry. The most recently published include *The Hunger Moon* and *Made in Detroit*. She lives with her husband in Well Fleet, Massachusetts. *(margepiercy.com)*

Martha Postlethwaite has spent her professional life listening to and sharing stories as a minister, counselor and spiritual director. She is a contemplative with a heart for the inner journey. She loves to read and write. On many occasions, a poem has been enough to save her.

Claudia Rankine is the author of six collections of poetry, including *Just Us: An American Conversation*; *Citizen: An American Lyric*; and *Don't Let Me Be Lonely*. She has also co-edited several anthologies, written three plays, and collaborated on numerous videos. Among her awards and honors are the Bobbitt National Prize for Poetry, the Poets & Writers' Jackson Poetry Prize, and a long list of fellowships. She lives in New Haven, Connecticut, and teaches at Yale. *(claudiarankine.com)*

Laura Ann Reed, a San Francisco Bay Area native, taught modern dance and ballet at the University of California, Berkeley before working as a leadership development trainer at the San Francisco headquarters of the United States Environmental Protection Agency. Her work has appeared in numerous journals and anthologies in the United States, Canada, and Britain. Her chapbook, *Shadows Thrown*, was published in February, 2023 by Sungold Editions. She and her husband live in the Pacific Northwest. *(lauraannreedpoet.com)*

Rainer Maria Rilke (1875-1926), born in Prague, traveled widely in Europe, with Paris serving as the geographic center of his life until World War I. Thereafter he lived in Germany and finally Switzerland. By the time he died of leukemia, his work was intensely admired by many leading European artists but was almost unknown to the general reading public. Today he is universally regarded as a master of verse.

Alberto Ríos's most recent works are *Not Go Away Is My Name* (poetry) and *A Good Map of All Things* (novel). Recipient of the PEN/Beyond Margins Award, Western Literature Association Distinguished Achievement Award, a Rocky Mountain Emmy Award, and a finalist for the National Book Award, Ríos teaches at Arizona State University. He is Arizona's inaugural Poet Laureate, a recent chancellor of the Academy of American Poets, and director of the Virginia G. Piper Center for Creative Writing.

David Romtvedt's latest book of poetry is *No Way: An American Tao Te Ching* (2021). Past poetry titles include *The Tree of Gernika*, *Dilemmas of the Angels*, *Some Church*, *Certainty*, *How Many Horses*, *Moon*, and *A Flower Whose Name I Do Not Know*. He has also published fiction, nonfiction, and translated works. He served as Wyoming Poet Laureate (2003-2011) and is now emeritus professor of creative writing at the University of Wyoming. *(davidromtvedt.com)*

Gary Earl Ross is a retired language arts professor from the University of Buffalo/Educational Opportunity Center. His published works, which are mostly prose, include the short story collections *The Wheel of Desire* and *Shimmerville*; the children's tale *Dots*; the historical novel *Blackbird Rising*; and eight stage plays, among which is *Matter of Intent*, winner of the 2006 Edgar Allan Poe Award from Mystery Writers of America.

Rumi (1207-1273), with poems in this volume translated by Coleman Barks and interpreted by Daniel Ladinsky, was born in the region known today as Afghanistan. A Persian-language poet, Muslim scholar and teacher, and Sufi mystic, he lived most of his life in present-day Turkey. Barks, who has described him as "one of the great souls, and one of the great spiritual teachers," says that Rumi "wants us to be more alive, to wake up . . . . He wants us to see our beauty, in the mirror and in each other."

Marjorie Saiser's *Losing the Ring in the River* (University of New Mexico Press) won the Willa Award for Poetry in 2014. Her most recent book, *The Track the Whales Make*, deals with ways love goes right and goes wrong. It is in Ted Kooser's Contemporary Poetry Series at the University of Nebraska Press. Her poems have been published in *Poet Lore, Midwest Quarterly, I-70 Review, Rattle, Verse Daily*, and "American Life in Poetry." *(poetmarge.com)*

Pat Schneider (1934-2020), poet, playwright, and librettist, is the author of ten books, including *How the Light Gets In: Writing as a Spiritual Practice* and *Writing Alone & With Others*, both from Oxford University Press, and five books of poems. Founder of Amherst Writers & Artists, she was for thirty years adjunct faculty at Pacific School of Religion in Berkeley, California. Her last book of poems was *The Weight of Love* (2019).

Ellie Schoenfeld is the author of three collections of poetry. Her work has appeared in an assortment of anthologies, small press journals, and on *The Writer's Almanac*. She has participated in many projects working with artists from various genres and worked with regional literary organizations on community poetry projects. She has been the grateful recipient of ARAC/McKnight fellowship grants and served as the 2016-2018 Duluth Poet Laureate.

Heidi Seaborn is the author of *Marilyn: Essays & Poems* (2022), *Give a Girl Chaos: See What She Can Do* (2019), and three chapbooks. Her work has appeared in over 100 journals, including *American Poetry Journal, Beloit Poetry Review, Copper Nickel, Cortland Review, Missouri Review, december, Financial Times of London, Greensboro Review, Nimrod, Pedestal, Penn Review, Mississippi Review, Tar River Poetry, Tinderbox Poetry Journal, Yemassee Journal*, and *The Slowdown*. She is Executive Editor of *The Adroit Journal*. *(heidiseabornpoet.com)*

Sohrab Sepehri (1928-1980) was an Iranian poet and painter who pursued his creative aims while working in several government agencies and traveling frequently outside his home country. Among his published works were *The Water's Footfall*, *The Traveler*, and *The Green Volume*. In 1964 he resigned his government position to focus on the arts, deeply informed by a variety of spiritual and poetic traditions. His poetry remains so popular among Iranians that he is known simply by his first name.

Maggie Smith is a freelance writer and editor. She is the author of *Goldenrod* (Simon & Schuster, 2021), *Keep Moving: Notes on Loss, Creativity, and Change* (Simon & Schuster, 2020), *Good Bones* (Tupelo Press, 2017), *The Well Speaks of Its Own Poison* (Tupelo Press, 2015), *Lamp of the Body* (Red Hen Press, 2005), and three prize-winning chapbooks. Her poems and essays have appeared in such publications as *Best American Poetry*, *The New York Times*, *The New Yorker*, *The Paris Review*, *Ploughshares*, *The Washington Post*, and *Guardian*.

Thomas R. Smith is a poet and teacher living in western Wisconsin. His most recent poetry collections include *Windy Day at Kabekona: New and Selected Prose Poems* (White Pine Press) and *Storm Island* (Red Dragonfly Press). He has also edited several books, most recently *Airmail: The Letters of Robert Bly and Tomas Tranströmer* (Graywolf Press). He teaches at the Loft Literary Center in Minneapolis and posts poems and essays at his website. *(thomasrsmithpoet.com)*

Holly Wren Spaulding is the author of *Between Us* (2022), *Familiars* (2020), and *If August* (2017). St. Brigid Press put out a special edition of *Fire* in summer 2021. Her debut chapbook, *The Grass Impossibly*, received the Michigan Writers Cooperative Press Award for Poetry in 2008. Spaulding's writing has appeared in *Michigan Quarterly Review*, *Witness*, *Poetry Northwest*, and elsewhere. She is the founder of Poetry Forge. *(hollywrenspaulding.com)*

Kim Stafford is a writer in Oregon whose mission is "to raise the human spirit." He has taught writing in dozens of schools and colleges in the US, and in Scotland, Italy, Mexico, and Bhutan. He founded the Northwest Writing Institute in 1986 and co-founded the Fishtrap Writers Gathering in 1987. He is the author of a dozen books of poetry and prose, including *Having Everything Right: Essays of Place and Singer Come from Afar*. He served as Oregon Poet Laureate (2018-2020). *(kimstaffordpoet.com)*

Kansas-born **William Stafford** (1914-1993) published more than sixty-five volumes of poetry and prose, beginning with the award-winning *Traveling Through the Dark* when he was forty-eight. In 1970 he held the position now known as US Poet Laureate. For more than thirty years he taught at Lewis and Clark College in Oregon. His personal ritual was to compose a poem a day. *(williamstaffordarchives.org)*

Ron Starbuck's three collections of poetry—*There Is Something About Being An Episcopalian*, *When Angels Are Born*, and *Wheels Turning Inward*—follow "a mythic and spiritual journey that crosses easily onto the paths of many contemplative traditions." He has been a contributing writer for *Parabola Magazine* and has published work in *Tiferet: A Journal of Spiritual Literature*, among other places. He founded and operates Saint Julian Press to promote interfaith and cross-cultural literary dialogue.

Julie Cadwallader Staub lives and writes from her home near Burlington, Vermont. Her poems have been published in literary journals and anthologies, including *Poetry of Presence: An Anthology of Mindfulness Poems* and *The Path to Kindness: Poems of Connection and Joy*. Her poem "Milk" won the 2015 Ruth Stone award. Two of her poems have been nominated for the Pushcart prize. She has two collections of poems: *Face to Face* (Cascadia Publishing, 2010) and *Wing Over Wing* (Paraclete Press, 2019). *(juliecspoetry.com)*

Christine Stewart-Nuñez is the author and editor of several books, including *The Poet & The Architect* (2021), *South Dakota in Poems: An Anthology* (2020), *Untrussed* (2016) and *Bluewords Greening* (2016), winner of the 2018 Whirling Prize. Her poetry has been the basis for cross-artistic collaborations with musicians, choreographers, visual artists, and architects. You can find her at the University of Manitoba where she teaches in the women's and gender studies program. *(christinestewartnunez.com)*

Maya Stein is a writer, poet, and workshop facilitator living in mid-coast Maine. She has kept a weekly short-form poetry practice, "10-line Tuesday," since June 2005. She is the author of two collections of personal essays, three collections of poetry, and several writing prompt guides. Her most recent books are *Grief Becomes You* (2019) and *The Poser: 38 Portraits Re-Imagined* (2021). She is Editorial Director of Toad Hall Editions (toadhalleditions.com), a small press and publishing service. *(mayastein.com)*

Joyce Sutphen's first collection of poems, *Straight Out of View*, won the Barnard New Women Poets Prize. Her recent books are *The Green House* (Salmon Poetry, 2017), and *Carrying Water to the Field: New and Selected Poems* (University of Nebraska Press, 2019). She was Minnesota Poet Laureate from 2011-2021, succeeding Robert Bly, and she is professor emerita at Gustavus Adolphus College in St. Peter, Minnesota. *(joycesutphen.com)*

Heather Swan's poetry has appeared in such places as *Terrain, Poet Lore, Phoebe, One Art, The Hopper, Cold Mountain Review, Midwestern Gothic*, and *Edge Effects*. Her poems have been included in anthologies such as *Healing the Divide, Rewilding, New Poetry from the Midwest*, and the *Center for Humans and Nature Kinship Series*. Her book *A Kinship with Ash* was published by Terrapin Books in the fall of 2020. She teaches at UW-Madison. *(heatherswan.net)*

Rosemerry Wahtola Trommer co-hosts the *Emerging Form* podcast on creative process, Soul Writers Circle, and Secret Agents of Change (a kindness cabal). Her poems have been featured on *A Prairie Home Companion*, "American Life in Poetry," *PBS Newshour* and *Oprah Magazine*. Her most recent book, *Hush*, won the Halcyon Prize for a collection on human ecology. Since 2006 she's written and shared a poem a day. One-word mantra: Adjust. *(wordwoman.com)*

Lynn Ungar is a poet, Unitarian Universalist minister, and dog trainer who lives in Vancouver, Washington with her two Australian Shepherds. Her books of poetry include *Bread and Other Miracles, Breathe*, and *These Days: Poems of the Pandemic Age*. *(lynnungar.com)*

Laura Grace Weldon has published three poetry collections: *Portals* (Middle Creek, 2021), *Blackbird* (Grayson Books, 2019), and *Tending* (Aldrich, 2013). She was 2019 Ohio Poet of the Year. Laura works as a book editor, teaches writing, and maxes out her library card each week. *(lauragraceweldon.com)*

David Whyte grew up in Yorkshire, England, with a strong, imaginative influence from his Irish mother. He now makes his home in the Pacific Northwest of the US. The author of eight books of poetry and four of prose, he holds a degree in Marine Zoology and has traveled extensively, including working as a naturalist guide in the Galapagos Islands and leading anthropological and natural history expeditions in the Andes, Amazon and Himalaya. *(davidwhyte.com)*

Ruby R. Wilson is a poet and writer who has published three poetry chapbooks and is co-editor of both volumes of *Poetry of Presence*. In addition to capturing images with poetry, she is also a photographer and loves roaming the countryside with her camera. She lives in rural Brookings County and is an archivist in the South Dakota State University Archives & Special Collections Department. *(rubyrwilson.wordpress.com)*

Wu-Men, or Wumen Huikai (1183–1260), was a classic poet and Chinese Chan ("Zen" in Japanese) master. He is best known for compiling and commenting on the koan collection *The Gateless Gate* while he was the head monk of Longxiang monastery.

Index of Authors and Titles

& So, 147
About Standing (in Kinship), 119
Ackerman, Diane, 100
Addition, 52
Addonizio, Kim, 63
Adkins, Lucy, 57, 152
Adolescent, 82
A few days after my first vaccine, 164
Ahmed, Dilruba, 39
Akers, Ellery, 155
Alcántara, José, 33, 37
Alien, 88
Allow, 53
Allowables, 81
An Apple Tree Was Concerned, 169
Anything, Everything, 48
A Pearl of Wind, 168
As You Fall Awake, 174
At the Cancer Clinic, 60
At the New Year, 56
August Morning, 35
A Valley Like This, 73
A Voice That Calms, 65
Baggett, Rebecca, 80
Basking, 34
Bass, Ellen, 114
Belonging, 167
Berry, Wendell, 157
Black Boys Play the Classics, 86
Blaeser, Kimberly M., 119
Blessing for the Light, 159
Blessing for Sound, 175
Breathe, 105
Can You Hear It?, 31
Careaga, Christen, 91
Champion the Enemy's Need, 101
Cherries, 49
Chorus from The Cure at Troy, 106
Clearing, 110
Clifton, Lucille, 84
Cold Solace, 130

Cole-Dai, Phyllis, *178*

Compassion, 122

Coomer, Jeff, *111*

Crews, James, *74, 78, 122*

Crooker, Barbara, *94, 139*

Dangel, Leo, *50*

Davis, Todd, *67*

Death, 133

DeDomenicis, MaryLisa, *87*

Derricotte, Toi, *86*

Detour, 146

Dierking, Kirsten, *32*

Divorce, 37

Dust, 41

Elephant in the Dark, 173

Erickson, Terri Kirby, *115, 123*

Every Mourning, 90

Excuse Me, 87

Farrell, Elizabeth Brulé, *77*

Faulds, Danna, *53, 172*

February 14, 63

Feeding the Worms, 137

Fehrenbacher, Julia M., *28, 150*

Feldman, Ruth, *146*

Figures, 79

Foley, Laura Davies, *68*

For Belonging, 177

For Everyone, 77

Forgiveness, 91

For the Man Whose Son My Son Killed, 102

For Warmth, 104

Fused, 64

Garcia, Albert, *35*

Gay, Ross, *54, 141*

Geraniums, 135

Gertler, Pesha Joyce, *38*

Giovanni, Nikki, *81*

Give Me This, 138

Glassmeyer, Susan G., *61*

Go Gentle, 129

González, Rafael Jesús, *109, 148, 149*

Good Bones, 140

Gorman, Amanda, *147*

Griffith, Lucy, *88*

Grunseth, Annette Langlois, *69, 113*
Halal Delicatessen, 96
Hanh, Thich Nhat, *104*
Harjo, Joy, *145*
Harris, Reginald, *97*
Heaney, Seamus, *106*
Heffernan, Gloria, *64, 120, 124*
Hennen, Tom, *26*
Henry, Nancy, *59*
Here Together, 70
Hesse, Hermann, *176*
Hicks, Patrick, *96*
Hilbert, Donna, *151*
Hirshfield, Jane, *108*
Hogan, Linda, *135*
Holding the Light, 158
House of Mercury, 93
How surely gravity's law, 171
How to Live Like a Water Lily, 69
Hughes, Holly J., *36*
Hush, 166
If You Knew, 114
Instructions to the Worker Bee, 57
In the Third Month of the Pandemic, My Husband Goes Through His Sock Drawer, 36
It Could Be, 28
I Tell You, 61
Joudah, Fady, *93*
Jump, 154
Kahf, Mohja, *144*
Kasdorf, Julia Spicher, *76*
Kaufman, Anna Belle, *130*
Kestenbaum, Stuart, *158*
Kleber-Diggs, Michael, *90*
Kooser, Ted, *60*
Ladinsky, Daniel, *65, 169*
Laméris, Danusha, *49, 137, 142*
Laux, Dorianne, *41, 79*
Lee, Li-Young, *44*
Lepp, Paula, *31*
Levine, Richard, *46*
Limitless, 172
Limón, Ada, *138*
Living in the Body, 116

Love and Fear in a Pandemic, 162
Love Elegy with Busboy, 42
Love Note to Silence, 33
Low, Denise, *117*
Luterman, Alison, *154, 164*
Macker, Teddy, *82*
McClain, Nathan, *42*
Merwin, W. S., *70*
Modlin, Brad Aaron, *51*
My Species, 108
Neighbors, 78
Nelson, Marilyn, *75*
Nepo, Mark, 168
New Bathing Suit, 123
Newcomer, Carrie, *52*
Nor'easter, 74
Normal, 97
Nuthatch, 32
Nye, Naomi Shihab, *43*
O'Donohue, John, *177*
Oliver, Mary, *27*
On the Day After You Left This World, 132
Origami Crane Tanka / Tanka de grulla Origami, 109
Orr, Gregory, *25*
Overheard, 141
Pandemic, 161
Passing the Orange, 50
Pastan, Linda, *129*
Patriotism, 136
People Who Take Care, 59
Phase One, 39
Piercy, Marge, *58*
Postlethwaite, Martha, *34, 110*
Potatoes, 152
Proxy, 124
Queens, 94
Rankine, Claudia, *85*
Redwood Dharma, *170*
Reed, Laura Ann, *174*
Remember, 80
Ribollita, 151
Rilke, Rainer Maria, *171*
Ríos, Alberto, *156*
Romtvedt, David, *66*

Ross, Gary Earl, *102*
Rumi, *173*
Saiser, Marjorie, *112*
Schneider, Pat, *99, 166*
Schoenfeld, Ellie, *136*
School Prayer, 100
Seaborn, Heidi, *30*
Sepehri, Sohrab, *71*
Sheltered in Place, 46
Shine, 160
Shoulders, 43
Slowing Down, 47
Small Kindnesses, 142
Smith, Maggie, *140*
Smith, Thomas R., *153*
Some Advice for Clearing Brush, 111
Spaulding, Holly Wren, *56*
Sponge Bath, 115
Stafford, Kim, *101*
Stafford, William, *73*
Stages, 176
Starbuck, Ron, *133*
Staub, Julie Cadwallader, *160*
Stein, Maya, *165*
Stewart-Nuñez, Christine, *162*
Sunday Morning Early, 66
Sutphen, Joyce, *116*
Swan, Heather, *127, 132*
Ten Thousand Flowers in Spring, 55
Thankful for Now, 67
Thank You, 54
The Aunty Poem (Mi Privilege Es Tu Privilege), 144
The Distance / La Distancia, 148, 149
The Dream's Wisdom, 75
The Gift, 44
The Healing Time, 38
The One and Only Day, 26
The Pedicure, 113
the river between us, 84
The Story Wheel, 145
The Wild Geese, 157
The Word That Is a Prayer, 155
To Be of Use, 58
Trommer, Rosemerry Wahtola, *126, 143, 167*

Trust, 153

Ungar, Lynn, *105, 161*

Untitled (Standing outside the conference room), 85

Untitled (You're invited to visit), 25

U Pick, 139

Walking with My Delaware Grandfather, 117

Watching My Friend Pretend Her Heart Isn't Breaking, 126

Water, 71

Weldon, Laura Grace, *48, 170*

We Were Made for This, 150

What I Learned from My Mother, 76

What It's Like to Fall in Love, 30

What Stillness, 68

What You Missed That Day You Were Absent from Fourth Grade, 51

When Giving Is All We Have, 156

when we get through this, 165

While the World Burned On, 127

Why I Smile at Strangers, 143

Why I Wake Early, 27

Whyte, David, *159, 175*

Wilson, Ruby R., *47*

Work Was His Religion, 112

Wu-Men, *55*

You Are a Poem with Feet, 178

You Just Never Know, 120

Your Birthday, 99

Permissions

The editors wish to thank the following publishers and individuals for permission to reprint. Every reasonable effort was made to identify and contact the copyright holders, procure licenses, and gather previous publication credits. We sincerely apologize for any errors or omissions.

About the Editors

Phyllis Cole-Dai began pecking away on an old manual typewriter in childhood and never stopped. Her work explores matters that tend to divide us, so that we might wrestle our way into deeper understandings of ourselves and others. She has authored or edited books in multiple genres, including poetry, historical fiction, memoir, and "musings." Her latest book is *Staying Power 2: Writings from a Year of Emergence* (2022). Other recent titles include *Staying Power: Writings from a Pandemic Year*; *For the Sake of One We Love and Are Losing: A Meditative Poem & Journal*; *Beneath the Same Stars: A Novel of the 1862 U.S.-Dakota War*; and, of course, *Poetry of Presence: An Anthology of Mindfulness Poems*. She has also published four music albums: *Beautiful Is the Moon*, *Friends*, *Child of All Earth*, and *'Tis a Gift*. Originally from Mt. Blanchard, Ohio, she now lives with her scientist-husband Jihong Cole-Dai and two cats in a cozy 130-year-old house in Brookings, South Dakota. Son Nathan, off at college, is her greatest joy. Join *The Raft*, her online community, at phylliscoledai.substack.com. Be sure to claim the complimentary gifts in her store when you visit phylliscoledai.com.

Ruby R. Wilson graduated from South Dakota State University with majors in German and Geography. She centers her work in the landscape and relationships that shape the world we all share. In addition to co-editing both volumes of *Poetry of Presence*, she has published three poetry chapbooks: *Campus Sketches: Images of South Dakota State University in Word and Photograph*, *At the Rim of the Horizon* (Finishing Line Press), and *Maybe the Moon is Falling*, one of four winners of the 2014 South Dakota State Poetry Society chapbook competition. She lives with her husband and an assortment of pets in rural Brookings County and is an archivist in the South Dakota State University Archives & Special Collections Department. Learn more at rubyrwilson.wordpress.com.

Acknowledgments

Our creation of this second volume of *Poetry of Presence* has been (like the first) part spiritual exercise, part labor of love, and above all, a gesture of kinship. We have special appreciation for the kind contributions of these folks:

First and foremost, the poets: For this feast of mindfulness poems, you did all the cooking. (As editors, we just laid the table.) Thank you, thank you, thank you for the sustenance. There's no bottom to the bowls.

Fred Courtright at The Permissions Company: You're simply the best at what you do. Deep bows.

Sasha Bosshard, whose beautiful image graces the book's cover: The swan's outstretched wings, captured by the eye of your camera, are a perfect visual metaphor for the poems in the anthology, given their "sheltering" spirit.

Ginny Connors and her team at Grayson Books: Thank you for this generous opportunity to publish another collection of mindfulness poetry, and for honoring our earnest desire to include more poems in this second volume that explore the "tough stuff" of relational or social mindfulness. We couldn't ask for a better partner in publishing.

Our husbands and children: You know well the special challenges we faced in creating this collection. We celebrate how you helped us persevere, in every way. Without you, this book wouldn't exist.

Finally, to our abiding friendship, the river on which we float. In the white water, we hang on, trusting that calm waters lie somewhere ahead. We're never disappointed.

Deep peace to all.

Complete the collection.

Poetry of Presence
An Anthology of Mindfulness Poems

Phyllis Cole-Dai & Ruby Wilson, editors

A popular anthology of more than 150 mindfulness poems, mostly by contemporary or recent poets, both acclaimed and lesser known. These poems call us to the Here and Now, and help us to dwell there. The Here and Now is all that truly belongs to us, and as the poets say, it's enough.

"If you choose one anthology, I say let it be this one for the amazement—for the voices that, surprisingly, will speak to what you want to find in yourself."

> —*Grace Cavalieri, host and producer, "The Poet and the Poem from the Library of Congress"*

You may also be interested in

Exploring Poetry of Presence
A Companion Guide for Readers, Writers, & Workshop Facilitators

Gloria Heffernan

Enrich your experience of the original *Poetry of Presence* collection with this able guide through its wondrous terrain. Perfect for individual and/or group use. Includes eight engaging reading strategies, fifty stimulating writing prompts, and a twelve-week workshop curriculum.

Exploring Poetry of Presence II
Prompts to Deepen Your Writing Practice

Rosemerry Wahtola Trommer

What might happen when you show up to the moment with a pen in your hand? This companion book to *Poetry of Presence II* is a guide for writing poetry as a mindfulness practice. It features eighty-eight thoughtful prompts to help you explore how you meet the world, even when (or especially when) it isn't easy to be present.

Both titles available through your favorite bookstore